Praise

'Every business owner should read this book. Whether you're flitting from one "ideal client" to another, attracting the "wrong" clients, or you just want more of your dream clients showing up, this book will become your Ideal Client Attraction bible.

It's full of little gems and helpful exercises to help you find the right client for *you*, the right offer for *you*, by staying true to who *you* are and focusing on who *you* want to work with, not just working with whoever buys.

Your ideal client is out there, ready to connect with the real you. This book gives you the exact steps to show up the way you want to, fully aligned and excited about attracting more of the people you love working with into your life and business.

It's going to be a must-read recommendation for all my clients.'

— **Susan Payton**, international bestselling author of *The Business of Stories*

'I already had her video courses. I had her podcast. I've even got her saved in my WhatsApp. Now I've got her in paperback. This is officially the full Helen Tudor experience. Bold. Honest. Real. This book doesn't sugarcoat – it slices and dices through the noise to help you attract clients who actually want to pay you.'

— **Paul Green**, founder, Client Funnels Ltd

'*Ideal Client Attraction* is a fantastic reminder that business doesn't have to feel like a battle. Written with warmth, empathy and wisdom, it's like having Helen sitting right next to you, chatting to you about your business. But don't be fooled into thinking it's just "chat". This book is a roadmap for creating a business that feels aligned, magnetic and profitable. It's packed full of practical exercises, guidance from the heart and powerful insights to help you align strategy with soul and light a fire in your belly. It's not about hacks, gimmicks, chasing clients who aren't right for you or grinding yourself into burnout – it's about connecting deeply with who you are, what you offer, and the clients who light you up. This book is a must-read for every business owner who wants to attract clients they genuinely love working with.'

— **Gillian Haston**, founder and coach, Gillian Haston Coaching

'Helen pours her whole heart into everything she does, and this book is true Helen magic! You can feel it on every page. She doesn't just teach client attraction. She awakens the deeper truth of who you're here to serve. This book is both a guide and a gift.'

— **Shari Teigman**, performance mentor and creative strategist

IDEAL CLIENT ATTRACTION

A Spiritual Practice

HELEN TUDOR

Rethink

First published in Great Britain in 2025
by Rethink Press (www.rethinkpress.com)

© Copyright Helen Tudor

All rights reserved. No part of this publication may be reproduced, stored in or introduced into a retrieval system, or transmitted, in any form, or by any means (electronic, mechanical, photocopying, recording or otherwise) without the prior written permission of the publisher.

The right of Helen Tudor to be identified as the author of this work has been asserted by her in accordance with the Copyright, Designs and Patents Act 1988.

This book is sold subject to the condition that it shall not, by way of trade or otherwise, be lent, resold, hired out, or otherwise circulated without the publisher's prior consent in any form of binding or cover other than that in which it is published and without a similar condition including this condition being imposed on the subsequent purchaser.

For my family, my reason for everything

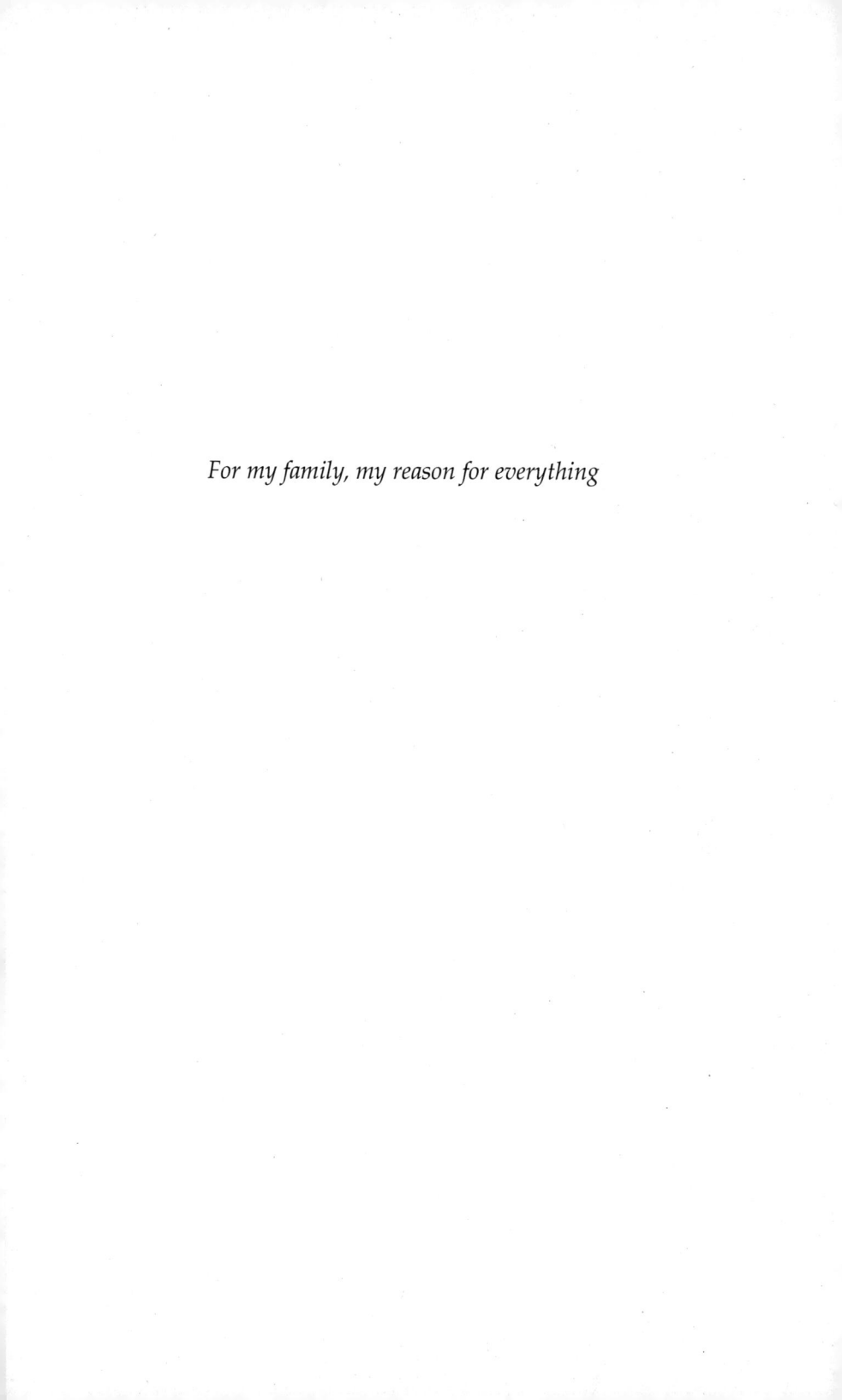

Contents

Foreword	1
Preface	3
Introduction	5
Are you ready to change your world?	6
My story	8
How this book will help	10
1 Bringing Best Client Energy	**15**
An invitation	17
Make or break	18
What does alignment look like?	22
When alignment is out	24
Future you	27
2 Strategy, Meet Soul	**35**
Above the line	37
Below the line	38
Left of the line is negative	41

	Right of the line is positive	42
	Self, offer and client	45
3	**It Starts With You**	**49**
	A lunchtime download	50
	Who are you?	52
	Dream big and be selfish	55
	Red flags and boundaries	59
	You are the magic wand	64
	Turn negatives into positives	69
	Listen to your soul	72
4	**Love What You Do**	**77**
	Avoid overwhelm from different offer options	78
	Say no to money like a pro	82
	Tailor it to you	84
5	**Love Who You Do It With**	**91**
	Why you need to create an avatar	92
	It's not supposed to be boring	95
	If they object, they're not your ideal client	98
	You owe it to your future self to do this	100
6	**Creating Your Ideal Client Map**	**103**
	Start by being specific	104
	Now give them a life	106
	Sad face	111
	Visualise them finding you	113
	Happy face	114
	The link between client and offer	116
	Create content with connection	120

7	**Meet My Ideal Client**	**125**
	Let's create Emily	125
	The stick figure of Emily	131
8	**Attract And Magnetise Your Ideal Client**	**139**
	Growth = engagement = sales	141
	The rings in your social media audience	142
	All strategies and tactics work	145
	Turn whining energy into winning energy	149
	Simple and free audience growth	152
9	**When The Going Gets Tough**	**159**
	Become unstoppable	160
	Be yourself – it's the best marketing hack	163
	My four pillars of content	166
	The minimum viable product	168
	Detach from the outcome	169

Conclusion: The Revolution Starts With You	**175**
Next steps	176
Acknowledgements	**179**
The Author	**181**

Foreword

I can't tell you how many times I've seen people, myself included, chase the next funnel, the shiny new tactic, or the supposed 'secret' to finally cracking client attraction. You put in the hours, you follow the steps, you do everything you're told, and yet the results still don't come. It leaves you doubting yourself, wondering if maybe you're just not cut out for this.

The truth, which Helen captures so beautifully in this book, is that none of those funnels or strategies matter if you skip the first step. And that step is knowing your ideal client at a level so deep that your message finally lands. That's the work Helen guides you through here, and it's the missing piece that makes everything else work better.

I know, because I've lived it. When Helen and I first sat down to talk about ideal clients, I had no idea how pivotal that conversation would be. But it became the foundation for everything we went on to build. Together, we generated millions in sales in our own businesses, and none of it would have happened without starting here.

What makes this book so powerful is the shift it creates. Instead of pitching at people and hoping something sticks, you learn how to truly persuade, not by pressure or gimmicks, but by showing your ideal clients that you understand them better than anyone else. And when that happens, they want to work with you.

That's the gift Helen has poured into these pages. Read this advice carefully, apply it fully, and you'll never look at client attraction the same way again.

Phil Harrison
Growth Strategist, Dark Mode Marketing

Preface

This book is for the action takers, the mission makers and the pure-hearted humans who are ready for more. More love. More joy. More money. More impact. More peace. More success.

This book is designed to amplify your greatness. It's here to create an inferno from the spark that's already inside you. It's the rocket ship to your dream life by design. It's here to change the game, fuel the revolution and rally the troops. Answer the call. Do not hesitate. Do not allow any shred of doubt to creep in. This book is meant for *you*.

The words on these pages will make you think and feel. Make you act. They're designed to activate you, to change you, to compel you forwards with clarity and purpose and joy. We will go faster and further together than alone. I've seen what's possible when soul and strategy align. It will blow your mind. Nothing will ever be the same for you again.

This book is an expression of my love for you and for your future. Do not read it unless you are ready to create a new story for your beautiful, precious, wonderful life here on Earth.

Introduction

If you're reading this, you likely want to attract more ideal clients. You may have attracted the wrong clients and wish to make this process easier and more enjoyable without starting from scratch. You want more success, more money, more impact. You want to work with high-value, high-paying clients who respect you and your work. You want to reignite your passion, feel inspired and have practical strategies to attract clients – or, better yet, for them to find you. You want to look forward to client calls with positive energy and feel uplifted after each interaction. You want to bask in the glow of your clients' successes and the positive testimonials you receive.

You want all of this, and have had all this, but not consistently. Non-ideal clients have made your world a darker place. You've dealt with clients where nothing you do is enough, causing self-doubt and even dread. You've felt sick at the sight of them on your calendar, deflated from your work with them and anxious about what went wrong.

You sense a disconnect between who you are and who you want to be. You're not fully aligned, like jigsaw puzzle pieces that don't quite fit together. Something feels off, and you can't see the full picture. You're unsure whether to start over or if a simple adjustment will suffice. You know you're a good person doing meaningful work, but there's a whisper from your soul indicating you're meant for more. This both frightens and excites you. You want guidance through this unsettling transition.

Are you ready to change your world?

The process of self-discovery and alignment starts today. By picking up this book, you've set the intention, and the wheels are already in motion. It's no coincidence that you're reading these words; there's a reason you're here with me now.

I know you are a good person here to do good work and have a positive impact on the world because I only attract those people. I don't teach Ideal Client Attraction, I *am* Ideal Client Attraction. I live it, breathe it, walk it and talk it. You are here because

INTRODUCTION

I attracted you here. Now you are here, my wish is for you to align your work with your true self. It's as simple as that.

You always have a choice. You can read this book and do nothing. Staying where you are will be equally comfortable and uncomfortable. This may not be the right time for you, and that's OK. You should be responding with a 'Hell yes', so only start the work if you're prepared to change your world. You can continue attracting a mix of good and bad clients, along with many mediocre ones – it's up to you. You can ignore that feeling that something isn't quite right and still have a financially successful business, or you can choose to accept the challenge of doing the work and achieving the results you desire.

Changing your world starts with attracting your ideal clients. Get this right, and everything else falls into place. Business feels good, money flows easily, and you experience real joy in your life. When you truly understand who your ideal client is, what motivates them and what attracts them to you and your work, you gain clarity. You don't suffer from confusion, overwhelm or indecision – the biggest obstacles to building a successful business. Instead, you make better, faster, bolder decisions. You instinctively know what to say online and offline to attract clients. You understand your audience and what they need to hear. You know where to invest your money and time. You know what to say no to and what to say yes to.

You can strategically and spiritually connect with your dream clients, who will bring you the money, impact and joy you desire. It's that simple.

Aligning to yourself, your offer and your client opens up a clear channel to manifest true success – not only money but good energy and a life that feels good rather than just looking good. Who you spend your time with in your business has the biggest impact on your mindset, which, in turn, impacts your execution of strategies and the energy in which you do so. You can improve your tactics and tech work so you understand your ideal client instead of feeling frustrated by them as they miss the mark over and over again and you start to blame yourself. Ideal Client Attraction is, without fail, the missing piece in every business that comes to me for help.

My story

In 2010, as a single mum burdened by debt, I never imagined I would build a joyful business that impacts thousands and generates millions. I had no money, no audience and no clear skills, and my goal was simply to earn enough to support my girls, repay my debt and avoid a job where childcare fees consumed my salary. I took it step by step, learning from mistakes while experiencing incredible moments.

INTRODUCTION

Today I run a successful group programme with over 2,000 students, earn more in an hour than I once did in a month and attract inspiring individuals who appreciate and uplift me. I'm invited to speak on podcasts and at events, and I collaborate with amazing businesses. I only take on work I love, at rates that excite me, and I decline anything that doesn't align with my values. I work few hours, enjoy ample time off to think and have a great team that lets me focus on what I love. I get paid upfront, am respected for my insights and am happily married with four children, living in a lovely area with my two cats and sausage dog, Dave.

I made my first million within three years of starting online and had my first seven-figure year in 2020. I've had £100K months, had £300K launches, won multiple awards, spoken on many stages and ticked almost every 'online entrepreneur' box on the bingo card. I have also made a million mistakes, been ripped off and let down, got in trouble with my finances, had business relationships go horribly wrong, attracted awful clients, had too many online dramas and got myself into all kinds of choppy waters along the way. Guess what? They were all due to one thing: a misalignment with myself, my offer or my client. When I am aligned, the flow state creates momentum and miracles. I have seen it and felt it and I know the difference. It's easy to make money, but making money in a way that feels good before, during and after the process is something else entirely.

More importantly I have trained, coached and mentored thousands of brilliant entrepreneurs in my community who have made zillions, attracted dream clients and smashed their online presence. I've tried and tested my Ideal Client Attraction methodology on many people in many situations – big and small businesses, introverts and extroverts, service and product businesses, practical and spiritual businesses – and I declare it battle-tested. It has improved every scenario.

How this book will help

Whether you're just starting out and deep in the hustle or you've been doing it a long time and want to do things differently, this book will help you reflect, realign and reignite your passion for the next step towards your dream life. I am so excited for you and what comes next.

I have written this book for you to hear my truth and learn my lessons. It will help you sidestep many lost opportunities, dead ends and difficult decisions. It will save you from difficult conversations, from dark nights of the soul and from spending lots of money on the wrong things. I want you to dream bigger, take bolder moves and get better results. This book is the start of you finding your way back to your truth, your passion, your joy. I have a beautiful, aligned life and I have written this book because I insist on the same for you. I want to be your inspirational mentor and

INTRODUCTION

confidant. This book is a conversation between us. I am here to hold your hand, be a friendly voice and gently push you out of your comfort zone.

I am giving it all to you because it matters. Now is the time to really lean into this opportunity, to see connecting with your ideal clients as a spiritual practice as the world hurtles into an AI and deep-fake landscape riddled with distrust and disbelief. Your clients are searching for you, but a version of you they can trust and believe in. Authenticity and honesty will be the USPs of the future. To truly understand and connect with your client is the superpower you need right now.

Read this book all at once or dip in and out as you need. Stop after every chapter and take copious notes in a pristine new notebook (I see you, stationery addicts), or scribble all over it with your new highlighters and pens. Why not get a friend or a group of business buddies together and work through it with each other?

Pick up what you love and drop anything you don't. I am not here to tell you how you feel about things and I am not here to tell you how to run your business. I am here to suggest radical self-awareness and radical self-love. Go gently on yourself. Relax. You have time. Take it easy and at the same time go forth and take action. You deserve the results you are going to get from doing this work. Don't hesitate. With an open heart, an open mind, let me help you help yourself.

I want you to take away one thing from this book: I believe in you, in your ability to change your world and create a business beyond your wildest dreams, doing incredible work with clients who bring you joy; I believe in your ability to give you and your loved ones a lifestyle you love. My mission is to help you make your business work perfectly, because you deserve it and, most importantly, your clients need you.

It doesn't matter what you do – it's how you do it that matters. When you bring your whole self to your business and align your strategy with your soul, with who you are, how you show up in the world and who you are here to serve, magic happens. I'm here to change the game by combining strategy and spirituality to support and serve your business, and you. It's nothing new – it's all there ready for you to access when you are ready.

What's gone wrong in the past is keeping the strategy and soul separate; once you realise how they are integrated as one complete support system for you and your business you will see how easy it can be to succeed. I have seen first-hand hundreds of examples of misalignment and hundreds of examples of alignment and it's usually easy to spot the difference. An aligned entrepreneur brings the joy to the work. They don't wait for the work to bring the joy.

In this book I am going to show you how to understand where you are at, where you want to be and how to step into a version of you that attracts ideal clients effortlessly. Then you can thrive in your business and go to sleep every night feeling happy, content and valued for who you are. You are a wonderful, unique, magical human being with so much love to give to yourself, your work and to others.

I am going to take you step by step through my tried-and-tested Ideal Client Attraction process. We will delve deep into who you are and what you are here to do; we will look at your current offer to the world and create an avatar of one ideal client. I will show you how the difference between strategy and soul matters when it comes to your business. We will look at how these two areas naturally and essentially support each other and why some strategies just do not work for you and your business, despite working for others.

By the time you have read this book you will have clarity, conviction and certainty on who your Ideal Client Avatar (ICA) is and how to connect and communicate with them to repel the wrong-fit clients and magnetise the perfect-fit people.

You will know what alignment means and how to achieve it by following the steps in the right order, no guessing and hoping.

You will have created an ICA map to be your everyday bible to refer to again and again to bring you back into a focused state in a distracting world.

IDEAL CLIENT ATTRACTION

You will understand that connecting with yourself, your offer and your client is a daily spiritual practice and be able to access it anywhere, anytime, anyplace in three minutes or less.

You will be motivated and inspired to show up online with a fresh perspective and renewed enthusiasm.

You will recognise your ideal client when they show up and be able to identify and remove wrong-energy clients before it is too late.

You will wake up every day knowing who you are speaking to and why and have a never-ending supply of content to post online.

You will have a simple daily plan of action you can execute then get on with your day, trusting that the universe will be meeting you halfway and sending those clients your way.

You will have an Ideal Client Attraction process that feels fun, effortless and magical.

You will have financial goals that feel exciting, achievable and inevitable.

Thank you again for putting your precious time, attention and energy into being here with me.

I appreciate you.

ONE
Bringing Best Client Energy

This chapter introduces the concept of best client energy (BCE) and reveals why understanding your own energy is the true foundation of client attraction.

The biggest misconception with ideal client work is that it is about the client. It is not – it is all about you. Who you are, what you want, how you best show up in your business. It's about your values, your boundaries and your red and green flags, and they are individual to you. It is fundamentally all about what makes you – and only you – feel good. Only you can go deep into your ICA because it is a reflection of parts of you on multiple levels. Ideal client creation is a magical progress and should be fun and light and enjoyable. Remember throughout that doing this process isn't like doing your homework and no one is marking it. It's for you and you only. Let's look at why it matters.

EXERCISE: Your best ever client

Take a moment to think about your best ever client. Bring them fully to mind. It doesn't have to be for the thing you're currently selling or even the business you're currently in. Think about:

- Who they were and what you did for them
- The experience of working with them
- What was great about them
- How they made you feel

Take a long, slow, deep breath. Feel how they made you feel. Swim in that energy. Savour it. Enjoy it. Connect to it. Now write it down.

You may have written things like:

- They made me feel valued, respected and like I matter.

- They made me feel excited, inspired and activated just by working with them.

- They made me feel so great, so happy, so proud of the work we did.

- They made me feel important, like what I had to say was worth listening to, that I knew my stuff.

- They made me feel like I made a difference.

An invitation

Now that you have thought about what makes a great client, I want us to hang out here for a moment.

Good isn't it? That's BCE and it's free to access; it needs only your intention and a minute of your time. I invite you to spend time every day in BCE because it will raise your vibration to a higher level and when you show up from BCE, guess what? Your posts, videos, talks, conversations and more will be infused with it and will draw people in. BCE is intoxicating and mesmerising to your ideal clients. I do want you to read the rest of the book but if life gets in the way, take this as a gift from me. My publisher will not be happy; I am way off-track already. I am supposed to be giving you teasers and trailers to get you to read on.

Now I want you to think about your worst client ever. Yep, the client that popped into your head when I asked you that. Think about what happened and how they were, and, you guessed it, think about how they made you feel. Write down the words. Ugh; the energy's nauseating, I know, but let's look at these. Things like 'They made me feel ignorant, useless, worthless', 'They made me feel like everything was a problem and nothing I did was good enough', 'I felt stressed, angry and upset' or 'I felt betrayed, let down, abandoned…'

This is worst client energy. We are not going to hang out here but you do need to be aware of it. When we feel triggered or upset by bad clients we often feel it's personal, which, of course, it is, and it can affect us on a deep level. It can also impact how we show up; I have seen extreme examples of a bad client fit causing mental health problems and even leading some people to stop being in business at all. That is so sad, as it's a problem that can be fixed at source, as you will learn in this book. Read on.

Make or break

Great clients can make you and bad clients can break you. I want you to know one thing: it's not you, it's them. There's no such thing as a bad client for all, but there can be a bad client fit for you. Sure, there are things you can do on a practical level in terms of screening potential clients, managing expectations and having better boundaries, but wouldn't it be easier if we changed the way we show up strategically and energetically so that we attract ideal clients and repel non-ideal clients just like a magnet? One way there's a pull, the other there's a recoil.

EXERCISE: The Client Traffic Light Audit

Another exercise that I do with clients is the Client Traffic Light Matrix. It's simple and, as always, should be fun and enjoyable rather than feeling like homework you keep putting off. Let's do this one quickly together.

Write out your last ten or so clients down one side of a piece of paper. Across the top, create five categories to rate the clients out of ten. These can be on a strategic level, like how good they are at communicating, how fast they pay, how well they implement your advice etc, or on a soul level, like how they make you feel, how you feel when you see their name in the diary or your inbox or how likely you would be to go for a drink with them. Mark everyone out of ten, with overall scores at the end. Mark your clients red, amber, green. Or soul suckers, soul neutrals and soul.

Now review each client and decide on your plan of action for each one.

Red clients: Sack them immediately or make a concrete plan to as soon as possible. No amount of money is worth dealing with this level of stress for your soul. The universe loves big, bold action. There will be a much better client along to fill their spot. Let them go with love and respect, but let them go.

Amber clients: What can you do to move them from amber to green? For example, increase your rates, have a difficult conversation about their commitment, or put some boundaries in place about how you communicate. A green client can become amber if they pay late, message you 24/7 or have unreasonable expectations, but if they have what it takes to be a green deep down – ie you like the person or the work you do together – then look at how you can influence change and go for it. Don't hesitate – send the email or message and turn your amber client to green.

Green clients: Show them some love. Tell them you appreciate them and why. Send them gifts, give them shout-outs online or post rave reviews. Open doors for them and bring them into your network. Green clients are usually green clients for everyone, so you have to work hard to show them you love and respect them and you can create client relationships that transcend what you originally agreed to do together. Don't wait – send that message of thanks and gratitude right now.

Now look at your worst client ever ('Boo! Hiss!') and your current or past red light matrix clients and answer these questions: deep down, was there a part of you that said yes when you meant no? Did you know you were compromising somewhere, somehow on something? Don't worry, it is not your 'fault' – it is common to take on wrong-fit clients because you are in need of something they have. This is usually money, but it can also be because they would look great in your portfolio, there is something interesting about the work even if you don't vibe with them, or even (this was me early on) because you feel sorry for them and want to 'fix' them only to find the problems are way beyond your scope or expertise. Either way, the bad client experience is something to be aware of and to avoid wherever possible.

I will caveat this with the fact that when you have no money all money becomes irresistible, as you have bills to pay and people to feed. I totally get it. I worked with many people for the wrong reasons when every penny counted. I just want you to have this awareness so you can take the money knowing there will be a trade-off down the line. Be prepared for it so you can deal with it and don't make it a personal problem. You're just doing what you need to do and that's OK. Let's work together to a future where you don't have to.

You may also (as I do) look back and think, *I just didn't know what I was doing in the early days when I took on all sorts of clients and projects that 'today me' wouldn't touch with a bargepole*, and that's OK too. You can only do what you can with the knowledge that you have at the time. Often it's all a great learning process to go through. The good news is that when you apply my process you can fast-track and leap-frog a lot of that and get to where you know who your ideal client is and how to attract them.

Working with ideal clients means looking in your diary and feeling excited to see their name. It means coming off calls feeling on top of the world. It means waking up excited for your day. It means being a better partner, parent, friend, customer in the coffee shop because you love your life. It means higher-paying, higher-value clients. It means more money and more impact and more joy. It means quantum leaps in your skills. It means more opportunities and more fun. It means limitless possibilities.

Ready for limitless possibilities? Of course you are.

> **YOUR TURN**
>
> Complete your own Client Traffic Light Matrix and take action. How good does it feel? You're beginning to take control and awareness is the first step.

What does alignment look like?

You can easily identify people you know who are in alignment and those who are out of alignment; once you start to see it, you can't unsee it.

Alignment with self is about knowing who you are as an individual and applying this to your business. This can be knowing and showing up in alignment with your core values, holding non-negotiable boundaries, trusting your gut instincts and working in a way you want to and that fits in with your life.

Alignment between offer and client are important and we will cover those in depth later, but alignment with self has to be at the centre of it all.

Someone once asked me, 'How can you tell if someone is aligned?' My answer was 'It looks like someone having a great time. It looks like someone excited to show up and do their thing. It shines so brightly it's impossible to look away. It is mesmerising, magnetic, intoxicating. It looks like someone who brings joy to the work, not someone who waits for the work to bring joy.'

As someone who is in complete alignment, let me tell you how it feels. It feels like a childlike curiosity for what's coming next. It feels simultaneously like both expansion and excitement and contentment and calmness. It feels like finally everything is good and there is no separation between who I am and what I do. It feels like I am doing what I was born to do. It's pretty cool. I want you to have it too.

I've worked with thousands of entrepreneurs through my challenges, masterminds and events and I can usually quickly tell if they are in alignment with themselves, their offer and their ideal client. I can read their energy but it also comes through in the way they talk about their business. An aligned entrepreneur talks with joy, excitement and confidence about who they are and what they do. They make you feel like you want to learn more, to hear more, and they want to tell you more. They are excited and passionate and lit up by what they do. If you are their ideal client, you will feel it. If not, you won't; in fact, you'll probably be repelled by them in subtle and not-so-subtle ways, and them by you. When the aligned entrepreneur meets their ideal client, it is an instant and powerful connection, and, of course, the opposite is also true.

> **YOUR TURN**
>
> When you're next at an event try and tune into those subtle energy shifts when you meet and talk with people about their business. Do they feel aligned to themselves and their offer, and do you feel aligned to them? Have fun with it and feel into it. You can't get it right or wrong; it's simply an observation.

When alignment is out

The ripple effect of misalignment is huge and not to be underplayed. It impacts every area of your business and your life. It impacts how you think, feel, eat and sleep. It changes the way you show up for yourself, your business and your relationships.

It feels like something is missing. Like there's a jigsaw and you have the pieces but the edges aren't quite lining up. Like you have a key in the lock but it just won't turn. Like you have a stone in your shoe and grit in your eye. It is irritating, uncomfortable and impossible to ignore for long.

You think you're doing it wrong but all strategies work, except when your soul doesn't want the results.

A mistake I see a lot is entrepreneurs starting businesses based on what they currently do rather than what they want to do. A broad example is HR directors becoming HR consultants instead of tuning into who they are and what they would love to do. They can make it work, and they're good at it, but the reasons they left follow them into their business and now they have the added stress and pressure of running a business. I also see a lot of ex-corporate high earners working twelve-hour days burn out and leave to start a business. They have the freedom to work when and where they want, but they sit at their computers for twelve hours a day instead of getting outside and out and about, working from anywhere, now they can.

I had one lovely client who was all set up to be a virtual assistant; she had done the courses, set up the website, done the LinkedIn profile and was ready to go. Nothing was working. She was posting, had a clear offer, was growing her audience and doing all the things I was telling her to do. Nothing was working. I got on a call with her and we talked through the steps of alignment and it quickly became clear that the last thing she wanted to do was boring admin work. She was doing it because that's what she could do and had done previously in jobs she had fallen into after school and college. She didn't enjoy being a PA but then set up a business being a virtual assistant, which is the same sort of work but with the added stress of finding clients and running a business. When we looked at what she truly wanted to do it was to help people and help people change. She retrained and became a hypnotherapist and now all the strategies that didn't work before work beautifully.

Another common misalignment I see is people chasing the money. They think that business is about making the maximum revenue and profit possible and don't think feelings and emotions should come into it. I'm sure you have heard the term 'it's just business', usually used by someone who has upset or mistreated another business owner, but it's much more than just business. There are a million ways to monetise your skills or create businesses that solve problems and make loads of money but only a few that truly align with who you are and what you want to do in the world.

When I was focused on LinkedIn and teaching people how to use it to get leads, I often found people wanted to work with me to get corporate clients for their soul-led businesses. For example, one client was a wonderful coach for high-performing women and worked one-to-one with clients, but she thought it would be better for her business if she worked with large organisations and had them pay for her services so the women got the coaching included at work. This is a great concept and works well for many coaches who prefer working that way, but when we talked through the differences in selling to corporates over individuals, the different ICA, the politics, the need to create a business case, the competition, the fact that the women attended the sessions because they were told to not because they wanted to and so on, it became clear my client wouldn't enjoy the process even though they were still the most fantastic coach. It truly is about what works best for you.

Somewhere along the way the message has got through that running a business is all about delivering what the client wants – that we get in front of people, find out what they want and deliver that at a price. What happens if we decide how we want to work and what we want to offer… and then find the perfect client for that? I see too many great people struggling with selling and servicing multiple clients in multiple ways and feeling overwhelmed and out of alignment as they struggle to keep up and keep everyone happy. I'm a huge advocate of creating the perfect offer for you to deliver, then finding the perfect client match, not the other way round. That way you are staying true to how you want to work and what you want to charge, and clients can accept or reject this and that is OK.

Future you

My friend is a big, important, consultant-type guy who has a long and distinguished career working with all the big brands and the big-cheese CEO types. We meet up for lunch and shoot the breeze on what we are doing in our own businesses, and I'd like to think we help each other think and talk things through. Last time we met he suggested we work together and bring a big transformational project to life for his massive corporate clients. He could open the doors and I could deliver the programme. We could make multiple six figures… Instantly, I could feel myself recoiling from the future vision of that.

Having to shmooze senior execs, getting onto preferred supplier lists, all the contracts and negotiations… the meetings about meetings about meetings… the corporate language… and that's before delivering it to people who didn't choose to consume it. No thanks. It's a full-body no from me on a self, offer and client alignment check. Some people would think I was foolish to turn such an opportunity down. Maybe I was. Maybe 'ten years ago me' would have sold my soul for six figures. I wouldn't put it past 'then me'.

EXERCISE: Goldilocking

You can use this yourself. I call it future-vision Goldilocking. Think about the opportunity in front of you, or create a hypothetical opportunity, or even imagine the future based on the success of what you are selling right now.

Go quiet. Take a long, slow, deep breath… and let it out… 'Ahhhhh'. I did that then with you.

OK, imagine this future. How does it look? How does it feel? Hot, cold, just right? Good or bad? Fun or boring?

Do you feel happy or sad, relaxed or stressed, joyful or miserable?

You can try on a few different scenarios and see how they feel.

I am going to future-vision myself first as a management consultant and then as a bestselling author of this book. Here we go: I take a deep breath, drop from my head into my heart space, put my hand on my heart and project myself into the future in two different directions.

Me as a six-figure management consultant feels all kinds of wrong. I visualise myself on trains, wearing non-stretch clothes and, horrors, high heels; in boardrooms; with screens; with bored people on laptops pretending to work but checking their emails and socials. I feel the loneliness of being away from my family in a nondescript chain hotel, the frustration when I have to wait ninety days plus as-long-as-they-can-get-away-with-it terms for payment; I feel the sadness of dropping balls elsewhere with my beautiful, perfect private clients and communities. I feel the misalignment of me in that environment. The one I couldn't wait to leave.

I see and feel the good too: the feeling of getting dressed for the day, nicely put together, without dog hairs on me or mud on my wellies. The thrill of leaving the dishwasher, the breakfast crumbs and obsessed-with-me-you-are-the-love-of-my-life-don't-leave-the-room-without-me Dave the Dachshund behind as I step onto the on-time fast train to London with the other grownups. The feeling of joy when a room full of forced-to-be-there, disinterested colleagues look up from their laptops in surprise as I talk to them like normal humans and get them to take action while we have a great day. The joy of big chunks of lovely money landing in my business account.

I Goldilocks it out. On balance it is not right for me. The self-sacrifice isn't worth the pay-off. It is not who I am and it is not what I am here to do. I can do it, I could do it and I am bloody good at it. I choose not to do it for my future self.

Now I do the same for my bestselling-author future vision.

Ooh, this is a good one. I am standing in front of the business books in WHSmith in Manchester Airport Terminal 2. I imagine what that moment will feel like. It feels so exciting. I am smiling widely. I can feel the emotion. I am close to tears. (I'm also tired and hungry as I have been writing solidly for five hours today, so that might be contributing. I am ready for a snack and some blanket time.) It feels like everything is vibrating on a higher level. I feel expanded – it's a miracle moment. I stand there with my family (we are on the way to Ibiza) and tears roll down my face as I soak in the moment. I am actually crying now. In a good way.

My teenagers probably wander off bored after taking a picture for their Snapchat with a 'Mum is crying in the airport what a loser' caption. Stu hugs me and says, 'Well done, babe. You did it.' I take a thousand pictures and tell everyone in the shop it's my book. I am giddy with excitement. I am going on holiday to Ibiza and I am a bestselling author. I did it. It also means that hundreds of thousands of people are buying and reading my book. That blows my mind. I soak it up. I feel an energetic connection with every single person who reads my words. Especially you. My life feels unreal yet incredibly real all in the same moment.

Dave sighs and rolls onto his back in bored amusement in the basket next to my computer.

I feel the hard stuff too. The sacrifice it takes to write. The risk of baring your soul and the pressure to fit your life's work into a single book to move people from where they are to where they want to be. The endless promotion, events, talking about it. The huge, and I mean huge, fear of judgement and negative reviews. The risk of laying it all out and the power of surrendering to the outcome. The risk of setting a goal and falling far from it publicly.

I Goldilocks it out. It's a no-brainer. The reward outweighs the risk for my soul. My strategy will be supported every day with my soul's desire for this outcome to happen. (Thank you so much for being a part of that manifestation for me. I appreciate you on a soul level.)

I enjoy hanging out in that future vision immensely, and I hope you have created a future vision for yourself where you have enjoyed hanging out. Feel free to journal on anything that comes up for you, and go there whenever you need a reminder of what you are doing it all for.

The power of alignment to what your soul wants to do cannot be underestimated. Listen closely to the whispers from your soul. To hear them you have to go quiet. There is no other way. Creating a daily ritual of connecting with 'future you' can only help you move in that direction, creating a sacred space to do so.

> **YOUR TURN**
>
> Make one shift today towards alignment. We call these micro-alignments. Small, subtle, yet powerful. For example, a micro-alignment could be turning down an opportunity that didn't feel right, re-affirming a boundary with a client or making getting outside once a day a non-negotiable. Write it down and keep writing them down – they all matter and they all move the needle.

Client attraction starts with self-leadership. When you show up anchored in the energy of your best ever client – confident, respected, excited – you become a magnet for more of the same. This chapter has given you permission to stop chasing, convincing or diluting. Instead, you align. You choose. You lead – and the right clients follow.

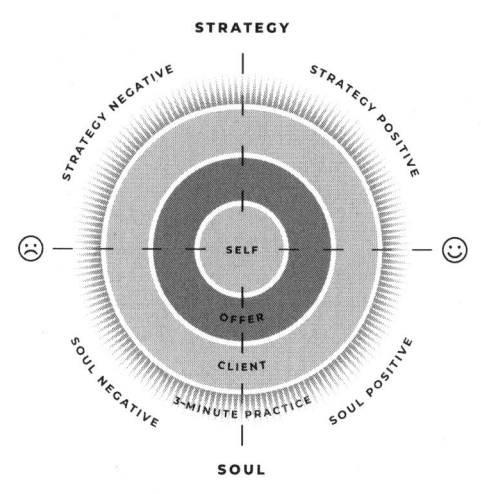

TWO
Strategy, Meet Soul

You can have the most beautiful offer, the boldest intention, the most aligned energy, but if the strategy doesn't support it, it falls flat. The same is true the other way around. In this chapter, we're going to bridge the gap between your soul and your strategy so the business you build works in flow with who you are.

There are many thoughts on what your soul is. I am no metaphysician, so I am going to go with my personal theory. It is who you are. It is how you feel. It is you on the inside. We will talk about 'soul negative' and 'soul positive' later in the book, but for now let's interpret 'soul' as the things we can't measure or even prove. Tuning into how you think and feel on an energetic level will support how you show up in your business (and your life).

For years I was 'The Strategy Person'. OK, actually I was referred to as the 'LinkedIn Queen', which initially made me cringe when people said it everywhere I went, then I just embraced it and wore headdresses and tiaras. I was famous for getting people *to do things*: take action, follow templates, do the work, be consistent, show up even when they didn't feel like it (especially when they didn't feel like it), do what they needed to do to get seen, get noticed, get visible. The strategy stuff. The above-the-line stuff in the illustration above.

I slowly realised that the spiritual and soul-led work I did with myself and my clients was not something separate from strategy but something essential in the integration of the person with the purpose and the productivity. It supports and directs the activity as well as the emotions, thoughts and feelings.

This was the breakthrough I needed in order to see the entrepreneur holistically and understand how this awareness impacted the results *and* the feelings about the results. Put simply, if your soul doesn't want it, your strategy won't work. Your soul knows what is best for you, whether you are conscious of that or not. This is the alignment piece.

The map in the illustration above is for you to see, at a glance, where you are at in terms of alignment. Let's look at the four quadrants more closely.

Above the line

Above the line is strategy. Up here are all the tangible things. Things that are visible, like money in the bank or conversions on a spreadsheet, social media posts, landing pages, videos – things that are out there in the world. They can be found, read, watched and seen.

Above the line is where logic and facts live. The vibe is real and measurable. This is where things are and where things happen. Irrefutably.

Above the line is also where things happen as a result of masculine energy. It's the doing, scaling, selling, pushing energy. It's the numbers, the data, the performance of your business as well as irrefutable things about who you are and who your client is. It is about how you (and your client) present to the world in ways that can be seen, touched and measured.

Up here are things like your website, offers, pricing and funnels, your current team members, freelancers and suppliers, your current bank balance and your latest post on Facebook.

So much good can happen above the line. It's also relatively easy to move the needle up here. You can usually implement new strategies or change your identity quickly and easily. For example, you could start posting daily on YouTube or dye your hair and change things in the 'real' world just like that.

Below the line

Below the line is spirituality, which is a different energy. It is all the things you cannot see, touch or measure. This is where our thoughts, feelings and emotions are. Down here is the feminine energy of being, allowing and balance. In a lot of ways the things below the line are indefinable and intangible. They are energetics, vibration and beyond all the things we can even put names to.

It is often a state of being or sometimes a reaction to something happening (above the line) which then impacts and influences our state (below the line), which then impacts and influences our next step above the line.

Here is an example. A client demands a refund, threatens to bad-mouth me on social media and sends long and endless emails to my support email inbox complaining about me, to me. I am not sure where she expects me to escalate those emails. This is all above-the-line stuff. She would like a refund. She would like me to know she doesn't like me. There is a threat of public drama if a refund isn't forthcoming. The team, usually wanting to keep these things away from me to protect my energy and keep me soul positive, have to admit defeat and let me know what's being said.

This impacts my emotions. OK, I lied, I am livid. Triggered to high hell. I tried to *help* this woman. I gave her more and more and more and it still wasn't enough. My team tried to help her. I am furious and upset and I feel rejected. I am feeling the unfairness so strongly it impacts my physical body. I rant. I cry. I rant some more. I send long, angry messages to my team about the unfairness of it all. I moan to my husband about it, who sends me back some soothing words but doesn't get into my drama energy with me. Most unsatisfactory. I consider somehow making it All His Fault. I talk myself down.

I have two options. I can use this soul-negative energy as fuel to my fire and get right above the line – reply to her email, threaten to post about her, feel the urge to write a post about how unfair clients can be to my legions of fans, who will jump into my comments and soothe me with their indignant agreement and thinly veiled rubbishing of this unnamed person in my passive-aggressive post that I know she will read…

Or I can wait. I am deep in my soul negative. How can I get myself across to my soul positive before I make a move above the line? How about blasting some music? I put on 'HUMBLE' by Kendrick Lamar followed by 'Get Back' by Ludacris and stomp around the office throwing some (confusing-to-the-dog) shapes.

Exhausted from the dancing, I go for a walk. The freezing air takes my breath away but wakes my face up. I crouch down and look at the ants and marvel at the way they are so strong yet so fragile. I look at the uncountable leaves on the trees and think about the abundance of nature. I stroke my cat, who is sitting in his favourite spot next to the warm Aga. I have a snack and a long, cold glass of water. I read some client testimonials. I feel a million times better.

I refund her and have her taken off all my email lists and out of all my groups. I get on with my day.

Incidentally, I used 'HUMBLE' as my walk-up song for the Women's Business Awards, mainly because I didn't think I would win and also because I like the song and didn't think it through. Picture me, wildly drunk on champagne in my emerald-green, slightly too long dress, surrounded by my team and best friends and sitting with my Oscars smile ready to clap for the winner, when my name is announced... the whole of the Blackpool Empress Ballroom erupts to 'Wicked or weakness', my best mate spins me round and then, as I get to the stage, 'Sit down, lil bitch, sit down' blasts out... Wow, this is awkward. The other nominees smile and clap me; everyone else chose

STRATEGY, MEET SOUL

motivational power songs like 'Girl on Fire' and 'This Is Me'. I still cringe a bit about that. Sorry, ladies.

Back to the map. Once you understand the map, you understand how to manage yourself. When you understand how to manage yourself, you can rule the world. I want you to rule the world.

Left of the line is negative

Left is pain, aggravation and moving away from where you want to be.

Above the line this could look like failed launches and funnels, less money in the bank than you would like, underperforming adverts, sales calls, webinars and events that don't convert but you don't know why, tumbleweed on your posts. It looks like investing in all the courses, programmes, mentors, tools, tactics, software and more but not getting results. It could be a lack of material things in your life or a run of bad things happening to you that are out of your control.

It also looks like procrastination. Whether that's endlessly writing in your notebook where no one sees it, tweaking your branding, sales pages or offers, or standing in front of the fridge eating ham out of the packet, sometimes you're not doing the thing you know you should be doing, because on some level you don't really want the result anyway.

It looks like a revenue plateau you can't break through and profits you can't increase. It looks like a misaligned team that doesn't deliver for you and clients that don't respect you or your boundaries.

Below the line this could feel like frustration, anger, sadness or hopelessness, jealousy, anxiety or fear. It could be feeling energetically flat or thinking negative thoughts about yourself or your business, sometimes to the extreme that you feel worthless, shameful or guilty. Loneliness is a common soul negative I see in entrepreneurs.

It feels like overwhelm, lack of clarity and blaming yourself or others. It feels like a sinking feeling of dread when you see certain people in your diary. It feels like rejection, humiliation and frustration.

It leads to a feeling of inferiority, of feeling like a fraud, of comparing yourself to others. It leads to blaming, shaming and attacking others.

Right of the line is positive

Right is greatness, aspiration and moving towards where you want to be.

Above the line this could look like oodles of money in the bank, launches that are predictable and positive, social media that gets results, high-converting events and calls, pillars of authority like a bestselling book, a popular podcast or multiple active platforms. It looks like a website that gets good traffic and produces results, a business that is scaling and growing with ease, revenue and profits that are all going in the right direction and an army of raving fans and positive testimonials and PR. You look great, sleep great and have all the nice things you could ever want in your life. You buy what you want and go where you want, without restriction.

Below the line this could feel like enjoying every day, experiencing gratitude and joy when you think of your business and clients, a sense of calm and peace when you are alone, pride and accomplishment when you hit your goals, love and appreciation for your clients and team members. It means feeling happy and present with your family and your friends, excited about the future and passionate about doing more in the world, feeling good in your body, mind and soul and allowing those good vibes to ripple outwards to the people around you. It means feeling aligned with who you are and what is happening above the line, finding glimmers of joy in the everyday.

I see many entrepreneurs looking outwards for the latest strategies, tactics, platforms and mentors instead of looking within to who they are and how they want to be in the world. Fundamentally, to have a business that is in misalignment with who you are will feel hard, challenging and like there is something not quite right even if it is performing well. Nothing feels as good as being in alignment does, not even millions of pounds in the bank. That's why it seems many millionaires feel lost and lonely. Something, somewhere has been compromised on their alignment with self along the way. Of course, we also see many broke people feeling lost and lonely too.

We want millions *and* we want joy and happiness. We can have it all. You can have it all, but what does 'having it all' mean?

To me it means living fully in alignment with yourself, your offer and your client, showing up with joy to serve others, feeling confident you are here to help them, and operating from a place of deep knowing that you are on the right track, in the right place and with the right people.

It looks like working with people you love and who love you. It looks like money in the bank and sales flowing easily. It looks like social media posts that connect to your ideal clients and never being stuck on what to say. It looks like showing up every day excited for more. It looks like a diary filled with people you can't wait to speak to.

It looks like an overflow of opportunities, a synchronicity of events and the magical appearance of the right people at the right time.

It feels like coming home. It feels enlightening and expansive and exciting. It makes you feel amazed at your manifesting skills and grateful to the universe for supporting you. It makes you want to shout from the rooftops every morning and curl up in a contented ball of happiness every evening.

It feels like you were made for this, born for this, are indeed this and this is part of you. It feels effortless and joyful and magical and wonderful. Even when things get hard in the day-to-day of running a business, you have a deep knowing that this is the right path and everything is worth it.

It does get to be that good, and more. It does get to feel that good, especially for you.

Self, offer and client

You can also see the three circles that represent the self, the offer and the client. These sit centrally to the strategy above, the soul below, the negative to the left and the positive to the right, creating the four quadrants. Each is important and influences the other, starting with the self and going outwards. Each area is intersected by the map and is in each quadrant. This is because all areas have the potential to sit in any quadrant at different times. The self stays central, as who you are on that core level doesn't really change.

The soul-positive and soul-negative quadrants are moveable and changeable, as our brains create stories about what is happening to us and we experience our thoughts, feelings and emotions. These are temporary and can be influenced by our actions. We can change how we feel and what we are thinking to be more positive by changing both our state (through moving, singing, hydrating, getting into nature etc) and our vibration (through gratitude, meditation, mindfulness, crystals etc). Remember: never make a permanent decision in a temporary emotion. Move yourself energetically first.

You can map where you are on the image to get a good overview. You can do this with anything in your business: your overall business, specific offers, clients, launches and much more. It's personal to you because one person's strategy positive (for example, 'Wahoo, there is £50K in the bank') could be another's strategy negative ('Oh shit, there's only £50K left in the bank'). It's a reusable tool that will change the way you think and feel about your business.

Through the rest of the book we will dive into the three areas and get specific on how to get all three circles aligned. As you will find, once we do this the magic starts to happen.

> **YOUR TURN**
>
> Where do you feel you are in terms of being strategy negative, strategy positive, soul negative and soul positive right now? Mark yourself on the map just for now, not forever.

Soul without strategy is chaos. Strategy without soul is empty. Where they meet – where your actions align with your energy – business starts to feel like magic. This chapter has helped you spot where you've been pushing from your head, ignoring your gut or trying to out-think your own misalignment. The answer is always to lead with your feelings and let strategy support your soul.

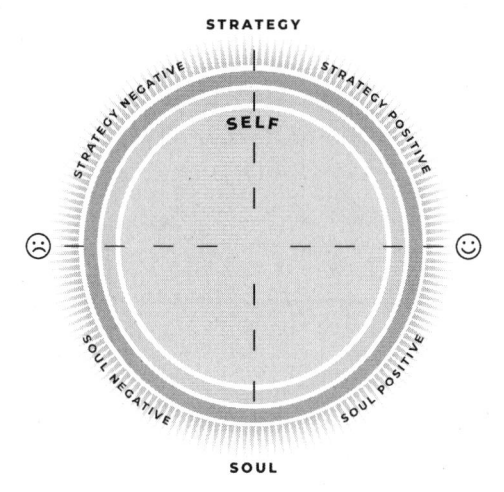

THREE
It Starts With You

If you've been trying to fix your business by tweaking your offers, changing your content or looking for the next 'perfect' strategy, this chapter is your turning point. Everything in your business starts with you: your dreams, your goals, your energy, your desires. Don't ever forget that.

Here's some good news and some bad news. The good news is it starts with you. The bad news is it starts with you. You don't just hold the magic wand – you *are* the magic wand. This transformation in mindset changes everything. Are you ready?

I wasn't ready for a long, long, long-ass time. I looked outside me for *everything*. I still do sometimes when I shift out of alignment: a new answer, a new tactic, a strategy, a tool, a tech, a mentor to make everything work. I ask ChatGPT for things over and over again. The irony is that when you get that feeling, that's your massive, waving red flag alert that you have slipped out of alignment: 'Yoo-hoo, it's me, your misalignment calling.' You feel you need something, anything to stop the feeling, and the feeling is itself sending you the signal to stop. To pause and wait. Breathe and go quiet. Go in, not out.

Sometimes, dear reader, I too get tired of taking the blame, being responsible for the world I see before me and the way that I feel. I get tired of knowing that I need to Do The Work some more. I get tired and I know you get tired. I know I sound like a faceless Instagram quote account but it is true: you have all the answers already within you.

A lunchtime download

I was midway through a spiritual VIP day when we broke for lunch (akashic record trips and energetic cord-cutting is hungry work) in my local gastro pub one blustery autumnal day, and that's when I got the vision for this book (and it's two sister titles to come) from nowhere. I was mindlessly chewing on my sourdough garlic mushrooms, with that green shoot stuff pushed to one side on my plate, and staring off to the middle distance when I got a neon sign in my mind's eye with the books and the titles brightly glowing out at me. I had no intention of writing a book, but my soul knew; it was just waiting for the quiet space to tell me. I could have ignored it – we have free will, of course – but I claimed it and put the wheels in motion. Step by step the vision came to life; it must have if you are reading this. It's magical when you think of it like that. Isn't that everything we create? A vision we bring to life. Who are we to argue with what our soul wants?

What if we need only to get clear on our intention and then create space for our soul to deliver each inspired step along the way? What if we don't even need to get that clear? I set my intention to help people in their businesses, to teach more people how to make more money and do it in a way that feels good. That's not that specific, but step by step the world unfurls ahead of me; I just have to keep leaping when it feels good and the opportunity presents itself.

I'd like to share one more story because it happened to me *today*. I said to my team on the group chat, 'We need to get in front of new people, people who have never even heard of me before, brand-new audiences. We need to think bigger, bolder, braver because if we do the same things we get the same results.' Something like that, anyway, probably less eloquent. As I was typing, a WhatsApp message from one of my best mates in business who I've not spoken to for a while popped onto the screen: 'I've got a TV opportunity for us! Would you be up for it?' Of course I said yes, and, well, who knows what will come from it.

I try not to get too bogged down in the how. Actually, that's a lie. I lie awake obsessing over how the things I want to manifest might happen, and it makes no difference. They happen in the most weird and wonderful ways. If I did manage not to get bogged down, I would probably be more productive than I am scrolling reels about sausage dogs and military families being reunited. Not with each other, that would be niche. You know the ones where they've been away and surprise the family in full uniform somewhere random? Love them. Sausage dogs doing sausage dog things, obvs.

So if *you* have all the answers…

Who are you?

What comes up for you when I ask that question?

For me when I self-enquire 'Who am I?', I get this: 'I am a good person and I am here to do good in the world. I am smart and use my intelligence and understanding of the world to help others. I am kind and generous and open-hearted and I am here to share my experiences and insight.'

I would love to hear what you get when I ask you. To hear, you have to go quiet. I am going to bet you are surrounded by noise – outside in the world and inside in your head. Society is noisy. Technology is noisy. Other people's marketing is loud and in your face. We are bombarded all day, every day with messages to make us feel less than so we buy more. We scroll, we buy, we have, we do. More, more, more. More noise, more stuff, more everything.

I invite you to go quiet. As quiet as you can in the pockets of time you can carve out.

I get it, life is busy. My husband and I parent four older children, look after three pets, run multiple businesses, have work teams to manage, sports teams to coach, social lives to engage in and fabulous large families who love a party.

The thing is, the noisier your life is, the noisier your soul gets. Let's take a minute to work out who you want to be, what you want to do, what you're here to say and how you want to feel.

Be. Do. Say. Feel.

Gift yourself the space and grace to think about these.

EXERCISE: Want to earn versus need to earn

Let's take a breath together right now. A nice long, slow, deep breath right down into your belly. Drop those shoulders from up round your ears. Another breath. Relax.

Remember everything is a work in progress. You are a masterpiece and these things take time. You can't

IDEAL CLIENT ATTRACTION

get it wrong and no one is judging you. I am not going anywhere. We've got this.

Let's work out what you are aiming for here in your business. I want you to write down two numbers. One is your need-to-earn figure (NTE) and one is your want-to-earn figure (WTE). Your NTE is the amount you need to earn to cover your existing lifestyle, bills and the fun stuff you already do, to keep you the way you are accustomed to but as a solo person. If there's one thing I've learned, it's that financial independence is worth a hell of a lot of money. It's great if you have a lovely spouse, generous parents or a sugar daddy right now, but let's look at what you need to make in your business to cover yourself and any dependents. For ease, let's do a monthly amount and a revenue amount. WTE is your *next* target monthly amount to give you a mega uptick in lifestyle, give you a bigger, bolder, brighter life where you can have more ease and flow, more opportunities to do what you want, more experiences and more money to give to the causes you care most about.

Before you write down the numbers in your head, I want you to consider these two things:

- Have you played small here?
- Have you fallen into the 'just enough' mindset of 'I just need enough to... (get a bigger house, pay off my car, go on one more holiday a year)' and are therefore making a small, incremental jump?

Now, I know that putting three noughts on is not the answer either; sure, it's fun to think about being a squillionaire and I highly recommend it as a hobby, but if you set a WTE here that is so far away the line is a dot to you, then you are going to struggle to envisage yourself there – so go on, make it a bit bolder and braver before you write down that WTE number. Make it so your life significantly changes – that is going to help when you use that vision to keep you motivated when things get tough. Write down all the things that will change when you hit that income level, and all the people it will impact.

When we do this exercise live on a webinar or a 5-Day Challenge, it is fun to read the comments. I ask everyone to do this and also let me know what 'silly shit' they would buy when they had treated everyone else and got their life aligned to the new income. Answers have ranged from 'a horse and I don't even like horses' and 'a boat and I live miles from the sea' to 'a £50K koi carp' and everything you can imagine in between. The £50K fish was a new one, though. I didn't even know that was a thing. You buy them and ship them over from Japan and if they die, they die. I mean, imagine investing in a fish that is the equivalent cost of a small flat in North West England and it dies in transit. I love that it is a thing. How abundant – a pond that contains *millions of pounds of fish*. Sometimes I go quiet and think of the '£50K fish guy' and hope he realised his fishy dreams.

Dream big and be selfish

I'd love to hear about your list of things you would buy, the people you would help and the places you would go. It's unique to you; I've never heard the same list twice. Dream big and be super selfish. What makes *your* soul happy? Where will you go, what will you do, what big, bold, audacious dreams will you make real? You don't need to share it, not everyone will see the value in your list – but you do, and I do, so that's enough.

Why not make a collage of your list and put it where you work or on your phone screensaver to remind you why you are doing what you are doing every day?

Take that WTE number and put it everywhere you can see it. Change your computer unlock code and your phone password to it (although we all use our faces now, and maybe by the time you read these words we will be controlling our phones with our minds and this part will seem horribly dated) and have it on Post-it notes in your home, in your purse (ditto, maybe purses are extinct now) and in your car (or flying machine). I also suggest putting it on your fridge, although your family may grow a little concerned about you. If you don't care what they think, put it there because you'll see it every time you're eating ham out of the packet instead of doing your work, and then do as I do, which is to write my next goal on my mirror in eyeliner so I can see it every day when I am brushing my teeth and doing my hair. My family are used to it; in fact, my daughter has her own business now and I noticed she has made her own mini vision board in her home office. Of course she is much, much cooler than me and has her WTE target in neon on her little neon sign maker on her desk. I love that it is there for all to see and sod what people think. You go girl. Proud mum moment. My other daughter wanted 2 million views on Instagram and guess what? Yep, she got it. You get to set the goals that you want to hit. No one else.

Setting your personal goal is food for the soul and it must align with *you* – not what you think it should be or someone said it should be. It's what makes you excited and happy and expansive. Look at your WTE number and go quiet. Hold it in your hand or hold your hand over the number in your notebook and have the other hand on your heart. Does this number feel aligned with who you are? Write down anything that comes up. If it feels good, it's good to go.

Let's revisit the exercise 'Your best ever client'. First bring them to mind and now let's go a little deeper. What would you say made them such a great client? Write down a list of all the things that made them great. Go to town because we want to wallow in the best ever client energy here.

It could be the way they found you, how easy they were to work with, that they respected your time and/or expertise, their enthusiasm and action taking, their open mind, their massive... budget... make as big a list as you can. The more you write, the more will come. You can expand this list even more with additions such as 'which meant that…' or 'which made me feel…'.

For example, 'They showed up to every call on time and implemented everything we discussed. Which meant that they got fantastic results, which made me feel valuable. Which meant that they gave me a great testimonial, which meant that I could use it on my socials and attract even more great clients, which made me feel proud of myself. Which meant that we made the most of every call and I felt respected and they valued my time. Which meant that my work was amplified by them, which made me feel like I was making a difference.' And so on and so forth. Listing, expanding and looking closely at how they impacted you, others and themself by being a great client for you.

Now you have the insights into above and below the line, you can look at your list and see what mapped above and below for you. They're all positive, of course, but some are strategic, tangible things you can measure and some are thoughts, feelings and emotions you can't.

As you are starting to see, they are both equally important and both supported by each other. The soul underpins the strategy and the strategy sits atop the soul. Bringing them both together is where we get self-alignment.

Let's not go too deep into worst ever client energy, as we don't want to be mapping all over to the negative, left-hand side, but you will understand how they equally impact you for this person to become the first to come to mind when I asked you to think of your worst ever client. Rest assured that if you did the same exercise as above there would be strategy-negative and soul-negative elements in your list. The two can't exist without the other; they are of equal importance to us as human beings. Just because we are running a business doesn't mean we separate our thoughts and feelings from what is happening out there in the world.

Red flags and boundaries

Red flags and boundaries are important when it comes to aligning your self to your business. When you ignore red flags or allow your boundaries to be bent or, worse, trampled all over, your soul feels it the hardest. Your soul is where the feeling of red flags comes from. Call it your gut instinct or your intuition. Red flags are often a feeling – and this applies to business opportunities and first dates.

In business we sometimes ignore our intuition, our inner self calling out to be heard or even experiencing a full-body no when we say yes – because we have been conditioned to not let emotions come into the cold, hard business of business. I say bollocks to that.

It's about using all of our available gifts of mind, body and soul to constantly, mindfully, micro-align what we do and who we work with to what we want deep down. It's about listening to the whispers from within that say 'This person isn't who they say they are' or 'This project is going to suck the life from your soul' or 'This partnership will implode and it's going to be messy.'

Setting boundaries is hyper-important if you are to create an aligned business. They are easy to set and hard to maintain, in my experience. When you want to help as many people as possible it can be hard to say no to requests for free support and advice, or answer all the DMs or comments you get across all platforms. With paying clients it can be even more tricky because the expectations can be higher, so it is especially important that you tune into what you will and won't accept.

For example, I make it clear to my private clients that they can message me anytime, day or night. Got an insight at 4am? Send me a DM. Want my eyes on something but you forgot to ask and now it's Sunday afternoon? No problem, send it over. Just had a difficult conversation and want to vent to me but it's 11pm? I really don't mind. I want my clients to send what they want when they want, when they are in the energy of the thing, so I don't have a boundary on when they contact me. I have to press this home to them because human nature is to respect people's downtime (and sleep), but it's important to me, and the relationship, that they don't hesitate. As a side note, I love asynchronous coaching and mentoring. I only learned the word in 2020 and have been working with clients this way ever since.

What I do is set the expectation on when I will reply, which will be at a time to suit me within forty-eight hours. It's usually 4.8 minutes but that's not the point; I have made space for me, which is the priority, and my lovely clients know the drill. I have had my phone on silent since 2016, which annoys Stu because I can never find it, although he always insists on ringing it anyway when it's lost somewhere in the house.

Let me tell you about a whole host of boundary overstepping and a red flag parade that happened to me back in my agency days. I won't name them, but let's say they are a huge national company and I was thrilled when we landed them as a client. We were hired to work with them on their marketing. What I loved about this client was the comms director. She was about my age, super lovely and passionate about her work and the organisation and we hit it off right away. I think the 'sales meeting' overran as we got business out of the way and chatted about our work, our lives and so on.

It was a fun project: easy, enjoyable, frictionless. As we had been communicating on LinkedIn, we arranged to go for lunch locally under the guise of the project and on expenses, but long story short, as we talked more, it became clear she had big dreams and a vision for becoming self-employed and even writing a book but was trapped in her big corporate job. I do hope she is reading this. We are overdue for another lunch. Time went on and the project continued until I got a call from her. It was good news and bad news. The good news was that she had thought more and had decided to take the leap – start her own business and start writing her book. I was made up for her. It also meant my contact at the big company had changed. I went in for the handover, whistling as I walked, looking forward to a smooth transition and to seeing my now friend before she left.

The look on her face when I arrived in reception told me everything I needed to know. This meeting wasn't going to go well. The incoming head of comms was an imposing woman who instantly tried to intimidate me with her career history (who cares?) and stamp her authority on the project with some wild micromanaging. She spoke to me like a child while my friend looked at me apologetically. I brought the meeting to a close and left with my assistant trailing behind me.

I felt *all* the feelings. I was deep in my bottom-left quadrant. I cycled through the emotions in turn. I was in shock; I remember we sat in my car outside in silence before saying 'WTF just happened in there?' I started to drive and moved into anger – honestly, how *dare*

IT STARTS WITH YOU

she speak to me like that – then sadness, being gutted it had turned into this, and, finally, acceptance.

She had to go.

I dropped my assistant off and picked up my daughter from school. I rang and was put through. 'I am just calling to let you know we won't be continuing with the project. I will ensure an efficient handover to your team and assure you no further money is owing.'

Silence. Then her incredulous voice came through the car speaker: 'You can't sack us, we are [insert household name].'

'I just did,' and with that I ended the call, cranked up the music and took my daughter for an ice cream. I remember it was a hot day and I wound down all the windows (the convertible was a while away yet) and felt this incredible sense of freedom and happiness, which I now recognise as a micro-alignment back to who I was and what I was prepared to put up with.

Notice how there was no apologising, no explaining, no trying to convince her she was wrong or that it was unfair. I just did what I knew I had to do and, of course, that bold, brave move was rewarded by the universe with bigger and better clients, and she was a long-lost memory soon enough.

Holding boundaries is for you, not them. Don't let anyone convince you that your boundaries are any of their business.

You are the magic wand

What's your story? Let's write down your Netflix Series 1, Episode 1 story of you.

EXERCISE: The story of you

Grab yourself a piece of paper and draw a line with '0' at one end and 'Today' at the other. This is your timeline and where we get to see who you are and what brought you to this exact moment in time on this planet as this version of you with your personality, energy, experiences and empathy.

Mark on it the ups, the downs, the milestones, the significant experiences and, let's face it, the trauma and the triumphs in chronological order. From fainting and wetting yourself at primary school and everyone pointing (just me, then?) to starting your business and where you feel called, expand on the impact and how each event made you feel. I bet you have multiple mini crisis points (where you decided enough was enough and things had to change) and pivot points (where you went to the next version of you) along your life from birth to now. When I do this with clients, I want to know it all, above and below the line.

For example:

Event: I dropped out of uni and ran away to be with a boy with a Ford Sierra Cosworth (moonstone blue, original alloys) in 1998... which meant that I had to call and tell my parents, which made me feel scared and guilty because they had always seen me as academic but also made me feel excited and liberated and rebellious, which made me feel alive.

Crisis point: Having to do a random presentation to the class about my dad's job (?) with crippling anxiety and having a panic attack during it. I asked for support but this was 1998. I hadn't made any real friends and I was out of my depth in a city after my little village with its cobbles and church. I was sad and lonely and this presentation was the final straw.

Pivot point: I took a job in recruitment which was life-changing and set me off down the path to the work I do now. Working in an engineering office in my Tammy Girl skirt, white blouse and barely black tights, smoking Benson & Hedges and drinking Hooch at lunchtime, it was like my life began.

You can go as deep or as shallow as you like here. Simple bullet points are OK too. It is crucial that you see an overview of who you are, where you have come from, what you have been through and what makes you you.

This part of a session tells me everything I need to know about the person in front of me and it will help you see yourself in a new way too.

You are magnificent. You have been through so much. You have kept going despite it all. You have been given the gift of life and you have not wasted it. You are sublime. A masterpiece. A hero. You did all of this. You, with just you to truly support you. Sure, you have encountered many, many characters in your story along the way, and you have played your part in many other people's stories, but through all of that, from birth to now, your only constant has been you. You have had a rollercoaster of a life with all its glorious wonder and all its day-to-day minutiae and it's not over yet. You can choose to complete the rest of your timeline however you wish, and how exciting is that? You have so much love and support for you from this world you can see and all other dimensions you cannot. You arrive at these words in the perfect time, place and space for your story to continue from this point. It is all working out perfectly. It is all going to be OK; in fact, it is all going to be so good you can't even imagine it yet and that is OK. You are not meant to have all the answers – you simply need to go one step at a time.

This step in time is acknowledging who you are.

Documenting and witnessing and appreciating your life story will give you so much insight into why you do what you do – or don't do what you do. About why you will fight to the death about some things and barely acknowledge others. About why and how you react and what your triggers are and how you can use them as a superpower. About why you want to do what you want to do. You are now ready for the next chapter of your business and life.

My dad loves me so much, and I him; he features highly in many of my pivotal moments (usually picking up the pieces and/or giving me a lift somewhere) and he often says my problem is that I can't take criticism. He (as always) is right. I also take this comment as a criticism, so round we go, usually in the car, where I can't escape, a well-worn tactic from my teenage years. 'Who likes criticism?' is my argument, but he is right – I hate it.

As someone who is highly sensitive, finds all criticism emotionally painful and even sees gentle feedback as a personal attack, what did I do with these traits? Became an online entrepreneur, which, on the face of it, seems absurd.

I went full-on immersion therapy by putting myself out there for criticism and judgement all day, every day across social media, where every day people would disagree with me and want to debate with me in the comments. I used to take the bait. Every. Single. Time. If you're reading this and we had a row in the comments from 2016 to 2020, then I apologise. I saw everything as a personal attack and would go to great lengths to defend myself – my work, my ideas, my personality, my ethics, my clients and so on and so forth. I had this burning desire to convince everyone on the internet that my LinkedIn methods were the right way and I was the right person for everyone to work with. Jeez. I feel my adrenals sparking just thinking about it. I fought and fought every day, building my business and amassing a wonderful army of fans who defended my honour and a big list of people who hated me who I hadn't convinced to like me, after all. I remember impatiently waiting for my girls to finish their fish fingers one night so I could get away from the table and see what that random man from Swindon had replied to my reply on his comment on my post, and obviously get the last word in.

I made a lot of money because drama brings attention but it also brought a lot of clients who loved the drama and it started to spill into my communities and client list. Not good.

In 2020 there was a huge, ridiculous argument on one of my posts and one line got to me: 'We knew you'd react like this.' That was it for me. I instantly dropped the rope. Just stopped arguing with people online (I am human and do slip up sometimes when I am tired or hungry or something really, really grinds my gears – if you see me doing it, drop a safe word in the comments to remind me, maybe 'custard creams') and my whole life changed for the better. I made more money, felt more joy and led a peaceful life. I took my oversensitive nature and I channelled it into serving the people who agreed with me and wanted more of me. I focused on them and ignored the rest. I see posts that trigger me and I let them trigger me and get on with my day. I do not get drawn in. I focus on serving and sharing and showing up for the people who want to listen.

The purpose of that story is to show you that you, of course, will have your faults and perceived personality flaws and that's OK. I am sure some of the people on your timeline have pointed them out to you over the years, but you can become hyper-aware of the impact it is having on you – your self – and change the way you respond, because you will feel it if you go off-track.

Did I feel good on the inside arguing with strangers on the internet? Of course I didn't. I felt justified, I felt right and I felt proud for backing myself, but I didn't feel good. I felt triumphant in the moment when I got a word in, and soothed when my audience would come to my posts to support me, but mostly I felt angry these random people were taking my time, energy and attention from my family, and I made a choice to stop. I take steps to shield myself from the worst of the criticism (I don't read my Facebook Ad comments or even my support inbox and definitely not my *Daily Mail Online* comments) but I know that it takes me below the line to soul negative and it's up to me to get into soul positive before I make my next move. A singsong, a snack, a visit to the ants or hugging a tree, it's on me.

Turn negatives into positives

When you think about who you are, flaws and all, remember you can turn negatives into positives with self-awareness, practical strategies and by simply making the decision to do so. You do not always have to be the way you have always been. If it doesn't feel good, it is not in alignment. When it feels good, you have alignment with self.

Let me ask you a personal question. When you wake up at 4am and can't get back to sleep, what goes round and round in your head? It could be work stuff, family stuff, health stuff, reliving something you have said or done (maybe a decade or more ago – whyyy do those things keep popping up?), worrying about the future or a full-on existential crisis. Make some notes on what keeps coming up for you.

What problems have you got? Let's pick one for now, maybe a business-related one, and consider the following questions:

- How do you feel about it?
- What do you think about it?
- What do you say about it?
- What don't you want anyone to know about it?
- What's the one thing you wish you could fix about it?
- Who is impacted by it?
- What are you not saying out loud about it?
- How long have you had this problem?

- What have you done to try and solve this problem so far?
- What's the worst-case scenario if you don't fix this problem?
- How do you feel about the next five years if nothing changes?

Now imagine you meet someone who can solve this problem for you or with you. What does life look like in six months, twelve months, five years?

When you started your business you probably weren't thinking about how to solve urgent and important problems but about what you wanted to bring to the world, so you got busy with your website, logo and social media accounts for it. Understanding how important your problems are to you, however, and how wonderful it is when they are fixed or at least under control is an important step in the Ideal Client Attraction process. Doing the process for yourself shows you how deep the consequences can go and how far the ripple effect can spread. Think about how you've invested before to help solve problems in your life – from a great pair of shoes to purchasing a house, the impact is felt. The bigger and more urgent the problem, however, the more invested you are in solving it on a mind, body and soul level.

> **YOUR TURN**
>
> Think about times when you've had a problem and been ready, willing and excited to solve it with the right solution. Before we move on to your offer, think about the *big*, overarching problem that you are here to solve and your business is set up to solve. Knowing what you know now about your life so far, why did you choose to do this as opposed to all of the other ways you could show up in the world?

Listen to your soul

I am on a mission to make profound spirituality accessible for all, so without further ado let's get to it.

EXERCISE: The one-minute self connection practice

This is the first of the one-minute exercises that make up your daily three-minute connection practice.

You do not need any special places, rituals, crystals, candles or robes. You do not need to go up a mountain, chant a mantra or abstain from anything. Obviously, you can if you wish and I am a fan of most of those things personally (although not a massive mountain fan, since a school skiing trip) but they are not needed here; we are connecting you to yourself. You are right there. Right now. Anytime, anyplace. There you are.

This is simply an intention. A micro-statement of intent to connect to yourself that will take only a minute.

IT STARTS WITH YOU

Take a long, slow, deep breath: in through the nose and out though the mouth. Close your eyes and drop those shoulders away from your ears. Relax. Put your hand on your heart, drop from your head into your heart space, and simply breathe in and out slowly while setting the intention to connect to yourself.

Let any expectation go with your breath, in and out. Whatever happens, happens. Whatever you get, you get. Nothing is OK and everything is OK.

Ask yourself these questions:

- What am I here to do?
- Who am I here to be?
- What do I need today?

Whatever comes, comes. Could be words, sights, sounds, a feeling, a knowing, a physical sensation, could be nothing right now, maybe it will come later. You have done your part in opening up the channel.

Stay as long as you like, there are no rules. I call it the one-minute practice so you don't feel it's something you don't have time for. You have a minute, let's create a commitment to a daily devotional minute spent with yourself.

Look back through your Netflix Series 1 Episode 1 backstory of you. You deserve a minute a day to listen to what you need right now. I know you are giving, giving, giving all day, every day because that's who you are and I love you for it; all I ask is you spend a minute in reverence for yourself.

You can journal, you can write posts about it, you can tell the world about it, you can message me and tell me all about it (please do) or you can keep it a sacred secret to yourself. You can also think I am weird and this is silly and it will never work. I'm there for all of it. All I ask is that you continue to spend a minute with yourself each day.

The resistance to this is real, by the way. We spend our lives not going quiet, filling the spaces with social media, food, friends, work, shopping, doing, achieving, learning, creating – and that's just me. I won't change and I am not asking you to make some unsustainable lifestyle change – I am just asking you to be open to the idea.

Listen to the whispers of your soul.

Sometimes you don't need to have a one-minute practice, sometimes you just know. My wonderful client came to my house for a Mastermind Day, sat on my sofa and said, 'I feel like I am living someone else's life.' She was a top-of-the-range senior partner in a global law firm, having worked her way up. She had it all – the title, the authority, the respect, the accomplishment, the office, the package that gave her the car, the house, the handbags – and still she came to me, compelled to my house because she knew she was meant for more.

IT STARTS WITH YOU

Having trained as a trauma-informed coach, first for personal interest and then seeing how she could work with others, she was hooked on thinking about the impact she could have with her clients. Having 'done the work' on herself and her family history, she was ready to bring a whole new version of herself to the world. Her employer wasn't happy with her wanting to promote it on LinkedIn, even if it was to be delivered in her spare time.

'You'll have to leave your job,' I said. Her face was a picture. I don't think I've ever seen someone's jaw drop open. I said, 'Write your resignation now and future-date it and because I don't want you coming here to live when you can't pay your mortgage, let's build your business from now to replace at least some of your income between now and then.' I work with a lot of entrepreneurs and I knew that for her it was so important that she went all in, even though it was scary.

You know what? At the time of writing she has taken the big, brave, bold decision to leave anyway. I am in awe of her. I cannot wait to see what she does next. Leaving a life where you have such an entrenched identity and have worked so hard and so long to get there, with all the sacrifices along the way, to create a new version of your life that follows your heart and soul just because you know it is what you are here to do is impressive. She is a warrior. I'm forever cheering her on, forever cheering *all* of you on who make bold, brave moves. I see you.

> **YOUR TURN**
>
> What does your life *feel* like when you are fully in alignment? Take ten minutes to journal on what that means to you.

This chapter has been all about writing your story. Where you've been is as important as where you are going. It all matters. It all makes sense. It is all relevant. Do not underestimate the power of telling your story, over and over again. You inspire people just by being you. You do not have to show up and juggle – you simply need to show up as you. You are enough; in fact, you are more than enough. You are magnificent, magical and made for more. Think bigger, bolder, braver.

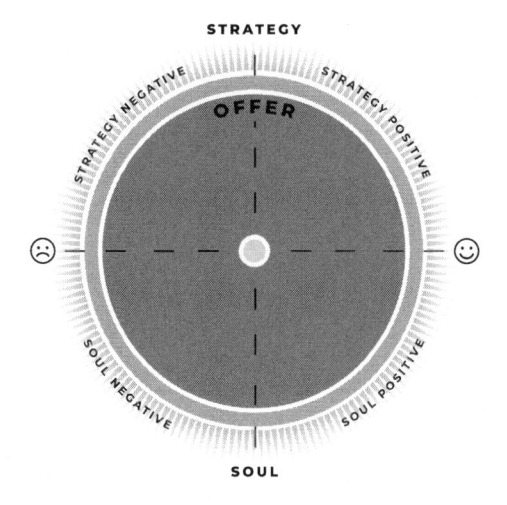

FOUR
Love What You Do

If something feels heavy in your business, there's a good chance it's related to your offer. In this chapter, we'll strip back the expectations and get to the truth of what you want to sell, and then you can work out who you want to sell it to. It's one thing having great clients, but if you're doing the wrong thing with them or hating what you do with them even if they love it, you're not going to love it. This chapter is about crafting an offer that creates the ultimate win, doing something you love in the way that you love to do it with clients you love to work with. This isn't some faraway utopia – it's real, it's possible, and I get clients to create these all day, every day. Once we get this piece right, everything else falls into place. You love talking about it, you love selling it, and, most importantly, you love delivering it. It's hyper-aligned with you, your soul, your client, their soul and their desired outcome.

This is the most important chapter in many ways, as it is what you are going *out there* with. It's the hook your client hangs their hat on, the pointy end of the wedge, the bullseye in their minds. Let's make it something you want to get famous for. From my experience of decades of doing this work with thousands of entrepreneurs, I can tell you one thing: there are a million ways to make millions, but let's make them in a way that doesn't suck your soul and make you hate your life. Let's make it something you love, which your clients love and which you're happy to show up and deliver over and over again. You're going to have to talk about your 'thing' a lot, in a million different ways, so make it something you love. Now you know how important your story is and what you're here to do, it's time to help other people with their stories. Go get another drink and settle in – this is important.

Avoid overwhelm from different offer options

Now let's get to it: your offer. What are you bringing to the world that people can buy?

I love talking in terms of offer rather than what you sell, because you can, and probably do, sell many different things. While we are here, let's talk about that.

If I ask you what you do, are you going to start reeling off all the different hats you wear, offers you have, ways to work with you and show me a dazzling array of price and package options? Will you launch into a weird, rehearsed elevator pitch that uses words you would never use in real life?

Often in business, we think more is more – more offers, more ways to work with you, more price points, more levels, more time frames, more options – when often, less is more.

Let's pick something to focus on – just for now, not forever. For the purpose of this book, from this point on let's focus on one thing, for one person, at one price. Now, before you slam the book shut or put down your Kindle in indignation at my affront to your passionate, multipotential, multidimensional entrepreneurial magic, please humour me. It is just for now – not forever. I am not insisting you only ever have one offer. You can come back and work through the steps with a million different offers, in a million different ways. All offers and events should have their own ICA for them anyway, but just for now, just for me, let's pick one.

Unlike picking a favourite child or deciding between curry or gravy on chips, I have a process for this. It is called the Value Joy Profit Model, affectionately known as my VJP. Much less interesting than it sounds, it is a tried-and-tested model of filtering offers, ideas and options to get quickly to your choice by process of elimination. As always, I also have a spiritual method of selection. You can use either or both – whatever works for you.

EXERCISE: The Value Joy Profit Model

Write out all your current offers and potential offers where you can see them. The name, price and a rough note on what is included. Don't get stuck here – as Nike says, just do it.

Sketch out a triangle with 'Value' at the top, 'Joy' bottom left and 'Profit' bottom right.

To decide what you are going to focus on, ask yourself the following questions:

- Where do I create (or have the potential to create) the most **value** in these offers?
- Where do I receive (or have the potential to receive) the most **joy** in these offers?
- Where do I make (or have the potential to make) the most **profit** in these offers.

For example, I love, love, love my group programme – it's a lively, loving community and it's my favourite place to hang out on Facebook. The programme offers lifetime access and the community is nearly ten years old. It started out as the LinkedIn and Business Mastermind, then we refocused it on ideal client attraction to allow us to concentrate on the work that is in this book, which, in turn, makes my LinkedIn strategies fly. I created it because I wanted a place that I would want to join and I would never want to leave.

I get a lot of joy from it. There is so much value in me being able to share my work with thousands of people and I have a much bigger impact than I ever could working with one client at a time. It is infinitely scalable and the profits are unlimited. It ticks every single box. This doesn't mean I don't love one-to-one client work with my heart and soul, but if I was going to pick one for this exercise, I would pick that. For now, not forever.

EXERCISE: The energetic selection method

There is a more energetic way to look at what you're offering and to assess all the things you could do, feel you should do, get asked to do and get told to do.

On the list of current offers you made in the previous exercise, cross off any that don't work for you. You know, the things you do and massively undercharge for or the things you charge well for but hate doing and get no joy from. Cross them right off, take them off your website, finish off all the last projects and never talk of them again.

With what you have left, focus on each one in turn. Take a deep breath, put your hand on your heart and close your eyes. Ask yourself:

- Do I love doing this?
- Do I want to do this?
- Is this aligned with who I am right now?

Your body will tell you. Lose the neutral and negative ones and keep the ones that feel the best – the ones where you add value, feel joy and make money, and which are aligned with you right now.

If you get none of them, it's time to take a few steps back and look again at who you are and what you are here to do. You get one wild and glorious life – spend it doing something you love. *You* get to choose what you sell.

Say no to money like a pro

Saying no to money is a large part of the evolution of your business owner mindset. Of course, when you're new, or broke, or both as I was, you just need to get some money in and that is A-OK with me. You might not know what you like to do, where your joy is, where you give the most value early on and that is OK too. Everyone feels that. Just draw the line in the sand now if you are still offering things you hate to do and undercharging and make today the day you *only* do things you love and get paid handsomely for.

It's your business. You make (and break) the rules. You get to decide what you are selling, how much you charge and how you deliver it. The client gets to accept or reject that. That's fine, but you don't run a business where you are completely at the mercy of what the client wants and how much the client wants to pay. Take control. Create offers that sing to *your* soul first, that fit in with *your* life and how *you* want to work at a price *you* want to charge. Take *that* to the market – don't let the market tell you how to spend your days or live your life.

I do get a fair bit of pushback on this: that it's not that simple, that all businesses are different, that I don't understand their market. I'll tell you this: I have never met a business that can't at least create sample offers with ballpark rates so the client can see exactly where they stand in the market. Pricing is a topic for another book because it is so caught up in money mindset, childhood, society, conditioning, fear of judgement, fear of rejection. It is deep below the line, in my experience. Putting your prices out publicly is above the line and takes around 0.5 seconds, yet there is a whole host of stuff going on below the line that influences it all.

My tip is to get your WTE number, divide it roughly by sixteen days a month (no one wants to be delivering five days a week), and that's your ballpark day rate. Alternatively, divide it by your offer price until you get to a number that feels easy for you to sell, or set a rate that makes you feel a little bit sick and a little bit excited and practise saying it out loud to the mirror until it feels more comfortable. Not to your friend or family member, as they definitely won't get it, but to the cat is fine. I used to charge £99 an hour; now it's around £1,000 an hour or more. No one can tell you what to charge, but please, please don't sell yourself short or compare yourself to others.

You are unique, you deliver amazing transformation – charge accordingly. There will always be people who can't afford you and that is a good thing; as long as you're delivering value for free elsewhere (through your content, your emails, your free training or however), you can sleep well at night. I have created thousands of hours of free content and you can get my advice for free everywhere you follow me. If you want my time and attention solely focused on you, it is going to be an investment. The more you charge properly to give you the lifestyle you want, the more time you will have to dedicate to creating free content, donating your time to charity and all the other good stuff.

Tailor it to you

The pro move is to create offers that are easy and fun and profitable for you to deliver and super impactful for clients to receive.

I had a client who worked with women to help them transform the way they think and feel about food and exercise so that they could lose weight and, most importantly, feel great. She was doing endless one-to-one calls and feeling burnt out, so we created a VIP day offer where instead of working with clients for twelve weeks for £5K she would charge £5K for an in-person day. Clients would love the intensity and impact of working through everything in one day and would go away motivated and excited for change. There would be light-touch support over WhatsApp for occasional questions or clarification and my client wouldn't be tied to endless Zooms in the diary; instead, she could schedule these full days and be more focused, which meant she would have more time for her family. She was also excited to get out from behind her screen and get dressed up and go into lovely locations in the city after years of working online only.

A different client might hate the thought of doing in-person days and love the flexibility of doing Zooms from anywhere in the world, or only want to work in an unstructured bra and stretchy leggings forever. We would build something different for them. This is why it's so important to get to know yourself and how you want to work. Consider the following questions:

- Do you love working in person or prefer online?
- Do you love group work or prefer one-to-one?
- Do you love working with organisations or individuals?
- Do you love working in short bursts with clients or developing long-term relationships?
- Do you love project work or working on a retainer?

- Do you love working on your own or do you prefer to have a team?

- Do you love working from home or do you prefer to be out and about?

This is all important. You can do *anything* with your day. You can make money from anything in the world. I can help you build a business doing whatever you would love to do in a way you would love to do it, but you have to look inside and get to know who you are and what your preferences are; otherwise, you are going to hate your life and we don't want that. Not on my watch.

EXERCISE: The one-minute offer connection practice

This is one way to stress-test an offer. You know the drill: deep breath, hand on heart and close your eyes.

Let's imagine you take this offer, read the rest of the book, create the most incredible ICA the world has ever seen, take my advice on how to attract them and sell all of these to all the right people. You achieve exactly what you have set out to do.

Fast-forward in time and envisage yourself living inside your goal, working with X amount of these clients delivering this offer and making £X.

How do you feel?

I did this exercise with a one-to-one client who came to me and said she wanted to create a culture transformation programme for corporates. We did the Netflix Series 1 Episode 1 exercise and it was clear she was an accomplished coach, consultant and expert in her field of how to improve communication. She explained how it was all mapped out on her whiteboard and had been for over a year, and how she was excited to work with me so I could help her with a strategy to take it to market via LinkedIn. We also talked about the personal challenges she had had along the way, including a significantly stressful experience over the previous year or so with one of her children.

We talked a bit about the offer and the programme and what that would entail. Her WTE was £30K a month and this programme was going to be £3K a month, so she needed ten clients. That was no problem; it's a simple process to map the ideal client, position someone on LinkedIn and then execute a marketing and sales strategy to bring them in.

Before we moved on to the next part, I surprised her by asking her to humour me and take a minute. I asked her to go quiet, take a breath, drop her shoulders, put her hand on her heart and close her eyes. I asked her to connect to herself and ask herself what she needed.

It came almost instantly: 'I need a break.'

IDEAL CLIENT ATTRACTION

'OK,' I said, 'I want you to move forwards on your timeline and drop into a future where we have done this session, you have executed perfectly, and you have sold ten of these programmes to dream clients. Now you are delivering ten programmes and making £30K a month. How do you feel?'

'I feel completely overwhelmed. So stressed, so worried about keeping everyone happy, so worried about doing a good job, I feel anxious even though I know I would do a good job.'

We came back to the session. 'What if we went back to the drawing board and you repositioned yourself as an executive coach. You would work with the CEO of these same teams but not deliver the whole programme. Ten CEOs paying £3K a month. Same money, ten hours a week or five if they prefer biweekly, offer support in between? How does that feel?'

'Wow, that feels light, fun, exciting, interesting. Relaxed. Spacious.'

We worked through some parts of shifting identity and how her experience, authority and skills made her a wonderful coach for CEOs, and that would allow her to have time in between for herself and her family, who needed her.

She knew she was an accomplished coach with a lot to offer but hadn't felt that was 'enough'. When we worked through the ICA map it became clear it was more than enough, and she was excited to share that offer with the world that same day, no whiteboard mapping required. Not forever, but for now.

If something has been on a whiteboard for over a year and no action has been taken, that tells me one thing: you don't really want it. It doesn't mean you will never do it. It just means that right now, it's not what you truly want. 'Future you' deserves to have an offer that makes you feel happy. 'Today you' deserves to have an offer you are excited to share with the world.

Now we have established what is right for you, let's check something important. Can you confidently deliver this with certainty?

One of the biggest problems I see is massive over-promising: people saying they will deliver complete life transformation, the moon on a stick and their first-born for one low price. A lot of people don't want massive change, because it scares them and/or sounds like a lot of hard work. People want change, for sure, and invest in it, but some of the best offers I see are simple and guaranteed. Do a quick sense check here to make sure your offer isn't overwhelming for your client to understand and you to deliver.

By now you should have your offer and be confident that this is the thing you want to sell *and* be confident you will be happy to deliver it. I'm excited that now

IDEAL CLIENT ATTRACTION

my job is to show you exactly how to create an ICA for it and attract those dreamy perfect ideal clients to you.

> **YOUR TURN**
>
> Choose the one offer you're going to map your ideal client to. Remember that every offer should have its own ICA, so write your offer out loud and proud – this is now your thing.

An aligned offer isn't just easier to sell – it's easier to love. When you love it, your dream clients will too. This chapter has given you permission to realign your offers with your energy, your strengths and your magic – because success only feels good when it genuinely feels good.

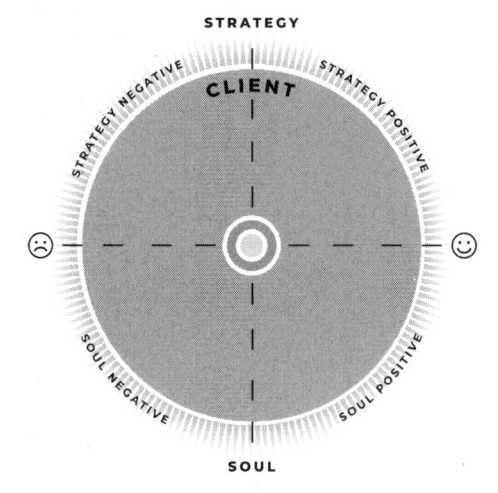

FIVE
Love Who You Do It With

This is the chapter where your ICA starts to emerge. You're not just figuring out who your ideal client is – you're defining what makes them a dream client on your own terms.

This is where the magic happens, things become much clearer, and you start to see the power in the work. You've understood how strategy aligns with soul, how you align with yourself and how your offer aligns with you. Now it's about making sure your clients feel and are drawn to that and you are sending out the right energy to attract those clients so that everything is working together and in alignment.

Grab yourself a drink and a snack because we are going to be getting *to it* in this one. This is my hard-core process. My deep work. My way of helping you bring it all together. This is more tried and tested than a Volvo Estate. Let's do this fresh, ready to work and with an open heart and an open mind. This is a meaty chapter and there is a process to follow. Go and get your pen and paper and no using ChatGPT. If I had to use my own brain and my own hands to write every single word of this book, you can do that too to work out your avatar. That's not to say ChatGPT can't be your best friend once you input your work into it. Honestly, it will blow your mind. AI only works on the information it is given, so when you give it your fully formed ICA map expect magical output.

Why you need to create an avatar

ICA work gets a bad rap. Even other marketers seem to enjoy saying it's outdated and irrelevant. It isn't. Well, not in my opinion, obviously, because I'm right here writing a bloody great book on it and you, my friend, are reading it. Go us!

It's great for you that a lot of people don't do ICA work, because now you do, and you do it my way: you have the secret weapon to creating content that speaks directly to your own special ideal client. In fact, don't tell anyone about this book, let's keep it between me and you. You will rule the world [evil genius laugh].

The most common mistake in ICA work is creating a bland, boring avatar that no one would want to work with, because you think that's who has got the money or the problem you'll fix. People get this so wrong because they forget to humanise them and create a living, breathing person with a soul, with hopes and dreams, fears and failures.

When you truly know your ICA and how they think, feel and operate above and below the line in all four quadrants, you never have to think about what to post or how to show up again. When you have mapped your client as a human and understood where they are and where they want to go, you can then see how they align with you and your offer. You can connect to them every day and you can refer to your map every day before putting pen to paper, thumb to phone, fingertips to keyboard.

Let's take this book as an example. Today I closed my eyes, connected to you in my heart and asked what you needed to hear from me today, which is what this book is all about. Everything I write is from my heart to yours. I am not sitting down to type on my big computer, drinking my peppermint tea, drinking water from my teenage daughter's ridiculously oversized dupe Stanley Cup from B&M, watching Dave chase the squirrels in the garden and thinking about what I want to say or what all the other people in the world will think of what I write today. I am thinking of what you need to hear from me today and I am writing that.

IDEAL CLIENT ATTRACTION

Everything I do, everything I say, every time I post, every time I put out an offer, every time I record a podcast or walk into a room, it's all about you and what you want. I tune into you and what you need to hear from me before I even get out of bed in the morning.

I know you need to hear that I know my stuff, that it works, that I am 100% confident it will work for you. I also know you want to hear that you are going to be fine, that you can do this and that I believe in you. I use this understanding of what you need to show up in devotion and in service to you. I want you to win with everything I have got, and my business is wholly focused on helping you get what you want. I am cheering you on every day and in every way.

As I write I can feel our connection. It is real and it transcends time and space, as in the future we are connected through this book. I am writing these words for you in the future. We are connected energetically forever. It's a billion-to-one chance we are both incarnated on the planet at the same time, and a billion-to-one again that you have found yourself with this book. A miracle in action. Here we are. I want you to truly feel my energy and my intention for you at this moment. I don't know where you are or what you are doing but I would love to know. This is our magical hotline to each other. Take a minute to breathe in and out and feel it. I'd love to hear from you; come find me on socials and tell me.

Welcome back. You can see I don't get overwhelmed and worried about what others may think because in my head, my heart and my intention it is just me and you. Two humans, *Mastermind* TV-show-style, chairs facing each other with spotlights picking us up in the darkness around. It's just me and you and I know you want me to get on with the book.

It's not supposed to be boring

Listen up. I have news.

ICA creation is meant to be fun. Yes, you heard it here first. It is supposed to be light, enjoyable, creative, expansive, inquisitive, joyful. A fun exercise you get to do to help you have clarity and to help your clients see you're for them. It is not supposed to be dry, boring, hard work homework that you have to do. That sounds the least fun ever. No wonder people 'sort of' do it or avoid doing it at all. It's much easier to believe you don't need to do it and merrily carry on with your day.

Funnily enough, I just took a lil' procrasti-scroll break and saw a post in my paid programme community from Sophia celebrating her new ICA map (OK she got a bit carried away and did twenty-two pages; you do not have to do this but if you want to, go for it) and how good she was feeling about her ICA now. This was some of the convo in the comments:

IDEAL CLIENT ATTRACTION

NIKI: Yes! It is great to get detailed about your ideal client. Like you I probably went overboard and to be honest I am currently half in love with my ideal client.

SOPHIA: I wanted to stay up and talk to mine all night – forget going to bed at 10pm!

SARAH: This is incredible! Well done you. I've got time aside this afternoon to work on mine – I'm actually excited to do it and I always used to dread it.

SOPHIA: There is massive FREEDOM in KNOWING that your ICA isn't an actual person but IS who you want it to be. I used to sit for hours wracking my brains on exactly who this ideal client was and if enough of them existed in this tiny, tiny world.

SARAH: Wow – it is so freeing to work on it from the perspective of who you want to work with, rather than who wants to work with you.

SOPHIA: Omg yes. Once we are attuned to WHO we want to work with and focus on only them, some of the people we don't really want to work with will back away like the guys in a bar who 'get the vibe' you are unavailable.

They get it.

I feel a lot of the resistance to doing the ICA work is this fear you will be not including people or turning away clients when you laser-focus on your one ideal client, or you will somehow miss out on business if you don't try to appeal to everyone everywhere all the time.

I understand. I would ask you to look back at your WTE number and your offer and work out how many people you need to attract to hit that goal. Many people only need between 10 and 100 great clients a year to create a fantastic business that gives them a great life, working with clients they love and who love them, doing work that matters and having time and space for themselves as well. Even at scale, I only need to attract 1,000 people a year to create a multimillion-pound-revenue business.

Now think of all the people in the world, or even just on Facebook or LinkedIn or Instagram. The people in your home town or in a Facebook group you hang out in. Search different job titles on LinkedIn. When I search I get 3.2 million people who identify as an 'entrepreneur', 2.5 million as a 'freelancer', 12 million as 'self-employed' and so on. I only need 1,000. You may only need ten. You are not trying to attract everyone and I do not want you to be out there attracting just anyone. You deserve better than that.

The other major misconception about Ideal Client Attraction work is that it is about the client. As you know, it is all about you – who you are, what you want, what you are here to do, the world you believe in, the way you are bringing your unique skills to the world in your unique offer – and then creating an ICA to fit that, not the other way round.

If they object, they're not your ideal client

Creating an ICA is a fantasy exercise. It is not based on a real person, because real people are flawed. You can create the perfect person in your imagination. Perfect because of who they are, the problems they have that you can fix and the fact that they are ready, willing and excited to work with you. You don't have to overcome objections with this fantasy person, you don't have to convince them to buy from you, they aren't comparing you with others; they are the dream client for so many reasons – and you get to choose them all. They don't exist in reality, so you can go to town making them the unicorn client of your dreams. Do not put limitations on them and do not play a small game here. Be bold, brave and audacious.

We create one next ideal client; we do not then say 'That is *it* – you shall never ever work with anyone who doesn't exactly fit this profile' because that would be silly. You will attract all kinds of people when you speak to your ideal client's innermost desires. You can change and review and renew and, hell, even redo your ICA anytime, anyplace. It is a moveable feast, a work in progress, a free-flowing creative exercise to have fun with. It will also change the way you show up in every area of your business. It's kinda a Big Deal.

At every level I have worked with – from consulting in a fancy oak-panelled boardroom in supple leather chairs around a built-to-intimidate polished oak table of comedic proportions talking to identikit men in suits about their global conglomerate right through to supporting anxious newbies stepping into the unknown world of self-employment with a side hustle – the first question is always the same: 'Who is your ideal client?' The response is almost always 'Anyone who…' or 'Women over forty who…' or 'Men who…' or 'Parents who…' or 'People with…' or 'People who want…'.

Anyone, women, men, parents or people are not an ICA. Having one that you can name and describe doesn't mean you will only work with that person or that you have to publicly declare you only work with that person. Ideal client work is different from having a niche. Having a niche is valuable, and getting famous in that niche is part of Ideal Client Attraction, but it is not the same as ICA work. Niching you do publicly as a marketing tool. ICA work you do privately as a clarity tool.

It would be a disservice to you if I said it didn't matter, because it does. Without an ICA in your heart, mind and notebook (and AI now), you are going to be talking to 'anyone who' and selling them 'anything that' and that is going to blend you right in with everyone else who does what you do. You won't be hitting those WTE numbers anytime soon. Sad times.

You owe it to your future self to do this

You owe it to your dream clients of the future, your dream business of the future and your future self to do this process now. It honestly shouldn't take more than forty-five minutes. Obviously, you might take longer because I am not there to ask you the questions with you answering as we go. You're going to have to be both me and you in the scenario.

When I do these co-creation sessions live we have Zoom recording us and AI taking notes, and I also take notes, allowing you to relax and settle into a creative space without worrying about remembering things. Here, you will be doing the version of notes that I do. You can also record yourself on Zoom doing the questions and answers and get that transcribed. The more the merrier because the more output you get, the more you can use it later on in the book.

Let's get back into who we are, what we are here to do and what we are here to sell. Get into the energy of yourself and your offer and future-vision you as the version of you who has already attracted your dream clients.

> **YOUR TURN**
>
> Spend some time connecting with that version of you. Draw on the BCE you tapped into right at the start of this book. Swim in it. Luxuriate in it. Love it and feel gratitude for it. Love yourself and feel gratitude for your bold, brave, beautiful self. Imagine your best client saying yes to your offer with excitement and delight.

The clearer your intention is to create your ICA, the easier it is to say yes to the right people – and no to the ones who aren't a match. This chapter has reminded you to raise your standards, trust your boundaries and attract clients who respect your energy, your value and your work.

SIX
Creating Your Ideal Client Map

This chapter isn't about marketing templates or demographics – it's about creating energetic resonance, knowing your person so deeply they would feel like you are reading their mind. This is about connection, not perfection. Get ready to create the most perfect ICA in the history of ICAs and map them directly to who you are, what you are here to do and how you show up in the world. It's time.

Draw a stick figure of a person to start. There's a reason for starting with the mental imagery of this person. I *always* start with this, whether I am doing this with a client one-to-one or on a flip chart on a stage or in a boardroom. I even draw one when I am doing an online masterclass and no one can see. Trust the process and draw one out.

Every time you answer a question about your ICA, the vision in your mind changes, so have fun with it and let's get to work. Remember that they don't exist and you are creating them just like you would if they were a character in a book or a film, so you can't say 'I don't know', because you definitely do – you're making them up. Decisions aren't always final, you can change your mind, but also it's important to keep moving through, as the quicker you answer the questions the clearer the picture becomes and the deeper the character becomes.

Start by being specific

The most important thing to remember is that the decisions have to be specific. You can't be 'around forty' or 'forty to forty-five' when you are a person: you are forty or forty-three or forty-five. It's right there on your birth certificate. The same applies to salaries. You don't have 'around six figures' on your payslip and you don't have 'corporate job' on your contract of employment. You don't have 'lives in the North West' on your post and you don't have 'maybe two children' in your house.

You're forty-seven, earning £97K working as a communications director at Barclays and living in Crewe. You have two children: Lyla, ten, and Matthew, eight. You're married to Dave, who is forty-eight and is an engineer who works away a lot and plays golf every Saturday, which drives you to distraction.

And so on. The specificity 100% matters. To create a character we can connect with, we have to create a human we can understand. Our brains can't understand demographics and maybe's and could be's and might be's. To create a person in our minds, we start with knowing exactly who they are and how they show up in the world: the above-the-line stuff. They are this, they do that, they have this. Then and only then can we go below the line to they feel this, they think that, they are worried about this. To truly understand our new imaginary best client, we have to set the scene.

The answers you choose are also interesting to me. Ask yourself 'Why is this perfect for me?' as you go. There is often a lot of you in your ICA, sometimes an old version of you, sometimes a desired version, sometimes none at all, but watch for the mirrors in this work, the echoes, the reflections, the shadows. Also gently check as you refine and reflect that you are not overlaying your own thoughts, feelings and fears onto your avatar. They are perfect for you, remember? They do have problems and concerns and challenges, and they are exactly the ones you can help them with. Look to create a perfect values match at every stage. This is the dream ideal client not just any old common or garden human client.

Remember the film *Weird Science*? They didn't create a random generic girlfriend – they created Kelly LeBrock. Remember that this is *one* potential ICA for your offer, not the only one. You can't get this wrong and no one is marking your work. It's not being carved in granite and it can be tweaked, changed, updated and scrapped and started again anytime. Relax.

Now think about what their name is. This is a weird one. Some people have a name that pops into their head straight away and we use that; some people get stuck. If you are stuck, or overthinking, or unable to think of one, I suggest choosing your favourite Spice Girl or member of Take That and going with that. Don't fall at the first hurdle.

What is their gender? Again, pick one. We are not excluding anyone – we are just picking one gender for this one person we are making up.

At this point I start to add some details to my stick figure, maybe some hair and a smiley face.

Now give them a life

Start to build your ICA's above-the-line life by answering the questions in the list below and writing all around the figure.

If the answer that comes in is 'I don't know, I don't care, it doesn't matter, this is ridiculous etc', then don't worry – that is the resistance to the breakthrough that's popping up. Resistance is real, and futile. Say hello and answer the questions anyway. Any time you feel that inner tantrum coming on, acknowledge it, breathe, relax and get back to making up your answers (to the ridiculous questions from the ridiculous woman in this ridiculous book [stamps feet]. Don't worry, inner teenager, I love you too) and moving through the process. Trust the process and go with it with an open heart and mind. If you're right and this is ridiculous then you will be right, and if I'm right and it's the breakthrough that is going to change everything and make everything in your business work better, you can be rich. You can be right or rich, you can't lose here. OK, onwards.

- What do they do for a living?
- How much money are they bringing home each month or each year?
- How long have they been doing their current job or business?
- What did they do before that?
- Why did they decide to make that move?
- What was their training or education like? If they went to uni, which one, what did they study, what did they get? Did they enjoy it?
- What was their childhood like?
- What is their relationship history? Are they currently in a relationship? If so, what is their partner's name, age, occupation?

- Do they have any children? If so, what are their names and ages?
- Where in the world do they live?
- What do they do for fun? What weird hobbies have they got?
- What does a date night look like for them?
- Do they play sport, watch sport or do their children play sport (or all three)?
- What did they used to do for fun but don't do anymore because life got in the way and now they miss it?
- What does Tuesday night look like for them? What does a Sunday afternoon look like for them?
- What do they do when they unexpectedly find themself with a free afternoon?
- How spiritual are they on a scale of a few crystals to month-long silent retreats?
- How environmentally conscious are they?
- What is their favourite place to travel to? Which holiday did they go on that they hated? Why?
- What grinds their gears?
- What's a hill they're prepared to die on?
- What's a world they believe in?

CREATING YOUR IDEAL CLIENT MAP

- Are they sociable? What sort of things do they like to do?
- Are they happy in their role or business? What would they change?
- Are they happy in their relationship? What would they change?
- How old were they when they had their children? How did their life change?
- How do they feel about their relationship with their children and wider family members?
- Have they got caring responsibilities? How does that make them feel?
- What labels do they assign themself? How do they feel about them?
- How do they feel about their finances?
- What do they look like?
- What's their story? What are they here to do?

And so on and so forth. This isn't an exhaustive or exact list – it is a flavour of the prompts I might give and the questions I would ask to build up a picture of the person we are creating.

As you answer, new questions will form, new directions will be taken, and your knowledge of this person will expand and deepen. You can go to town here. The more you ask and answer, the more you build, the more you flow and the deeper you go. Don't forget to have fun. The more detail you can go into the better. The more you write, the more you make space for new thoughts to come in, so just keep on going even if it feels a bit silly or like you might be going too far down rabbit holes describing them and understanding them. You won't be, I promise.

If you want to do one-word answers, that can work too. If time is short or you want to get it done, you can be efficient here too. This is your work to do your way; if you've had a go at it like I have asked, I am happy. Don't forget you can always come back to it anytime. I'm especially proud of you if you felt the resistance and did it anyway.

Now we have a strong overview of who they are and how they show up in the world, it's time to go deep on the problems they have that you can fix. As always, it doesn't matter if you sell a pair of shoes or clean houses; this process works. A great pair of shoes solves many problems, like not having the right shoe for the outfit, not feeling comfortable on a night out, not feeling confident walking into a room and so on. A cleaner solves many problems, like the shame of having people around, loss of time that could be used in the business, arguments between family members and many more things. In fact, cleaners are life-changing. Let's be honest. We love you.

Sad face

On your paper draw a sad face on the left-hand side and a happy face on the right side and a line down the middle. Here, we are going to focus on the sad face side, the problems your client has that you can fix (or at least help them with). They've got ninety-nine problems, like everyone, but let's focus on the ones that your business is going to help them with. You can use bullet points or long form, up to you. Here are some examples:

- What keeps them up at night? When they wake at 4am what thoughts are going round in their head about the problems you can fix?
- What are these problems?
- How do they manifest in their life?
- What specific examples of these problems are there?
- How do they feel about them?
- What do they think about them?
- What's the impact of the problems on them and others?
- What have they done about them so far?
- How much have they spent trying to fix them?
- What do they look at online to fix them?

- What happens if they don't fix them?
- How do they feel about the next five years?
- What are they not saying out loud about them?
- What's the one thing they don't want anyone to know about them?
- What's the worst-case scenario here?

Get specific. Ask yourself the questions and then ask 'which means that…' and 'which makes them feel…' to expand each one and go into deeper levels of understanding. Do a deep dive into the energy and impact of these problems on every level for your ideal client. Above the line with how they show up in the world and below the line with how they think and feel about their problems. Focus on and magnify every aspect to get a feel for where your client is in relation to the problem you can fix.

When you do this energetically you are meeting your client where they are, not where you want them to be. When you step into their shoes, into their heart and mind and into the darkness of the night as they lie there in bed, you start to see not only how important your work is for this person but also how necessary it is that you step up and show them you exist so you can help them.

It is not always doom and gloom. It can be a simple problem that is a niggle but is there and has an impact.

It could be that everything is going great but they want more, and how that frustration manifests in their life above and below the line. This isn't only about selling to pain points – it is an exercise to slip energetically into their skin and see the world as they do.

Now there is a break, a pause. A breath. Go on, take a nice, long, slow breath.

Visualise them finding you

Now imagine your beautiful, ideal client and their problems are minding their own business one day, just going about the day as normal, when they feel compelled to open up their phone and start scrolling. Like magic they see a post from you. It's a simple, short post that talks to one of their specific problems. They are mildly interested and give you a like. The next thing they see is a post from you talking about a client you helped who had a problem just like them. They give you a like and a follow. The next time they see a post with your current offer spelled out for them. What it is, who it's for, how it works and how much it is. They are interested so check out your profile and send you a DM. You start to talk.

It's a match made in heaven. They've got problems and you can fix them. They are the dream client and you are the dream person for them. You both like cheese and you get on like a house on fire. There is no friction and no objections to overcome. They can't wait to get started. They pay in full.

They do all the things needed, show up to all the things needed and take all the action needed. They surpass even the BCE we talked about way back at the beginning of this book. They make you feel ten feet tall, a million dollars and a better version of you just by them being your client. It is dreamy and magical and wonderful. You love to see them in your diary and their results feel as good as you getting them yourself. They have the full, no-holds-barred, nothing-held-back version of your work and get the most incredible results. They become your biggest fan, your number-one advocate and a banging case study. They refer all their similarly wonderful friends to you and you're living the dream.

Now fast-forward in time – maybe six or twelve months into the future, whatever works best for your business. You've worked together, done the things and got the results. What's life like for them now?

Happy face

Over on the happy face side let's list all the wonderful results and experiences and the impact of the work. How has life changed for the better? Again, expand on each answer by using 'which means that...' and 'which makes them feel…' to see the ripple effect. Your questions could include:

- Who is benefiting from the change?
- What's the best thing about the difference for them?
- What is something they weren't expecting but are thrilled about?
- How do they feel about making the decision to work with you all that time ago?
- What does the next year, five years, ten years look like now?
- How has this impacted other areas of their life?

And keep going.

You will feel an energy shift – from where you were deep in their problems, worries and fear to high up with their happiness, excitement, pride and relief. From feeling out of control to having someone come and help them get back in control. Spend some time here in this high-energy space. Where you can see, written out in front of you, the impact of your work on one human, you can truly see how you are here to change the world – their world.

I ask my clients at this point, and I ask you now, 'Do you think your offer is worth what you charge now that you see the shift?' I know your answer will be

'Of course it is' or possibly 'It's too cheap, I am undervaluing it', because when we step into and own the impact we have on one person at a time, we become priceless. Your offer is the bridge between where they are now and where they want to go.

Now we have spent some time luxuriating in how good we are and how important our work is to the world, instead of spending time scrolling through other people's posts and worrying they are better than us and we shouldn't charge so much and we will never find another client or whatever else we waste our time and energy doing sometimes, we can get to the crucial next step: mapping our offers and our souls to our ICAs.

The link between client and offer

Answer this question: what is it about your offer that they loved? Again, either bullet points or long form is fine. Expand each answer with 'which means that…' and 'which makes them feel…' to fully map the person with the offer. Answers could include:

- The way it's delivered
- Where it happens
- The insights they learn
- The people involved

- The systems, processes or tools you use
- The actions they take
- The energy and emotions involved

For example: 'They loved that the programme was all online, which meant that they could dial in from anywhere, which suited their lifestyle and how they like to work. This also meant all sessions were recorded, which made them feel there was added value as they could watch a replay' or 'They loved that the programme was all in person, which meant that they could have an immersive, intensive experience. They loved how it wasn't recorded, so they could really relax and open up without worries about it being around in the cloud.'

See how a different offer has different features and benefits your ICA responds to? Because this is a creative fantasy experience, guess what? Your ICA loves the way you love to do things too. How good is that? This is why we work out how you prefer to work first, then create an ICA who also loves that. When we show up in our wonderful energy for the things we love, we attract those who love the same things, because those are the things we focus on when talking about our offers. It's a beautiful, ever-increasing circle of visibility and client attraction.

Now for a key question: what is it about *you* they love? It could be:

IDEAL CLIENT ATTRACTION

- Who you are
- The way you show up
- The skills and knowledge you have
- Your energy
- Your personality
- Your patience
- Your honesty
- Your humour
- The way you are
- The way you make them feel
- The way you motivate them
- The way you inspire them
- The values you share
- The way you make them laugh

It could be anything, but dig deep and think about what you, as the person to deliver or sell them this, bring to the table. The whole of you, not just the one thing they are paying you for. Think about what people say about you and the words they use – they are rarely about the thing that you do. That you are competent at what you do is usually a given, but it's the way you show up and do your thing that makes you unique, and I want you to use this exercise to illuminate those aspects for you through the eyes of your

ICA. What would they say about working with you? If they kept a diary through the whole process, what would they write about you and your work together if they knew no one would ever read it?

Again, have fun with this exercise. You don't have to show anyone or type 'People love me because I am ace' on all your posts; it's more for you to know than for you to show. Think about those moments you have had when people are so full of gratitude for you being you and helping move them forwards. Get into that energy: where you feel valued and respected, where you're making a difference, where it's all high vibe and high fives. Harness it, because you're gonna need it.

Now think about why now is the right time for them to take action. What reasons do they have to make a decision to jump in now? It could be something you have influence over – like a deadline or the end of a bonus, a start date that isn't flexible or a limited number of spaces – or it could be something they have control over, like having to make a change, something coming up date-wise or personal reasons that mean now or never. It could also be something out of everyone's control, like the end of the year, a new term or a new government. There could be loads of reasons, but list some that make sense for your ideal client and your offer.

Finally, what do they need to do next? This is how they move towards you, come to your attention, step out from watching and waiting and make themself known. It could be send you a DM, click a link or fill in a form. Write it down.

How are you feeling about your ICA? I hope you love them. I hope you feel connected to them and see, feel and believe the impact your work will have on them. I hope you see just how important and unique you are in the process.

These notes create your ICA map and you can use them every day in your business. When you need an energetic infusion, revisit them and wallow in the amazing outcomes you deliver for your wonderful, perfect client. Spend time reading about how much they love you and your work. See exactly how your offer aligns with who they are and what they need. Sit alongside them in their problems and fast-forward to the future with them to their success. See and feel how important it is that you get out there so they can find you.

Create content with connection

Stuck for what to write today? Simply pick one thing off your map and use that to help you create a post. I use the pin-the-tail-on-the-donkey method: get the notes, close your eyes, whirl your pointed finger around over the page, then stab at anything. Open your eyes and wherever it's landed, use that as a jumping-off point for your post today. It could be about your ICA, about you, about your offer, about why now, about what next. It could be something from your Netflix Series 1 Episode 1 or it could be something completely random from the map. Don't overthink it and get writing.

EXERCISE: The one-minute client connection practice

Let's connect on an energetic and spiritual level with your newly created ICA. This is a big moment. Right now you get to truly meet with them, heart to heart. Follow these steps:

1. Set the intention to connect with your ICA. Take a long, slow, deep breath. In... out... Drop those shoulders. Close your eyes, put your hand on your heart and breathe.
2. Drop from your head space into your heart space, out of your head and into your body.
3. Connect from your heart space to your ICA's heart space.
4. Bring them into your awareness. You may visualise them, feel their presence or connect with their energy. You may see something, feel something, hear something or just have a sense of them. You may feel nothing at all; whatever you get is perfect.
5. Ask them 'What do you need to hear from me today, to make you feel safe that I am the person to help you with your problems?'
6. Wait a minute and see what comes up.
7. Thank them, disconnect from their energy back to yours and open your eyes.

IDEAL CLIENT ATTRACTION

Whatever comes, comes. There is no judgement, no pressure. Sometimes you might get nothing, sometimes it could be loads. It could be visions, sounds, words, feelings. Open up your phone and your social media app of choice, open a new post and write. Do not hesitate, do not second-guess, do not worry what people will think. Do not dilute the message. Whatever your ICA wants to hear, write it.

Each day relax into the practice and be open to what might come either in the moment or in another quiet moment later – maybe when you're driving or taking a shower. The intention is set, let the magic do the rest.

You can connect in with your client anywhere, anytime, anyplace. You don't need any special positions or an altar or any candles or crystals – although of course please do incorporate those things if you're feeling the vibe. Whatever works for you. I connect every morning before I start the day and sometimes before I am doing something significant, like writing this book, recording my podcast or thinking of ways to promote my offer.

It can take less than a minute and it can also take as long as you want. There aren't any rules; it's about the intention and the connection.

I connect with my ICA, Emily, and to make it more fun for me I always change the visual slightly. I bring gifts, like a new outfit, a new car or things like highlights for her hair or jewellery. I also change the setting. Sometimes we meet in Bali, sometimes in the woods, sometimes in her house; it's all just a bit of fun for me. It's a bit like those dolls where you would press out the clothes and hang them over the figure with little tabs. I have no doubt by the time this book is printing its tenth revised edition we will be having fully immersive holograms with AI built in appearing in front of us on command.

Just a side note on AI. At the time of writing this, AI is exploding onto the scene and I am sure it will feature heavily in all the strategies of the future. For me, this means this human-to-human connection will matter even more than ever. Energetics will become key and you showing up as you will be even more valuable than it is now. One of the fun things you can do with AI right now is put your ICA map in (even your handwritten notes as images) and then be confident you have put great input into it, which will mean you will get great output when you ask questions and give it prompts.

Well done on doing the work. Now you should know your WTE, your offer and its price, your ICA for it and a direct line to connecting energetically with them. You can then work out how many of your offers you need to sell to your ideal client to hit your goal. What is your number? Write it down.

Quick example: To reach my £10K a month goal for one of my businesses I need to sell ten £1K Ideal Client Attraction co-creation sessions per month.

IDEAL CLIENT ATTRACTION

Have a look at your mini sales and marketing plan and let's get to work. If you are into manifesting, you will recognise this is pure manifesting in action: setting an intention, making it clear, getting into that energy and feeling as if it has already happened. Now we surrender the rest to the universe and get into receiving mode. We also take inspired action every day and allow the universe to bring our ideal clients towards us while we create the bridge by growing our audience, engaging our audience and selling to our audience in some way every day.

I know this is a lot. This is as close as you can get to working with me one-to-one. You can watch a whole masterclass on this here: https://helentudor.online/booklink1

> **YOUR TURN**
>
> Turn the connections to your self, offer and client into a daily three-minute practice. The more you do it, the easier it will get, the deeper you will go and the more impactful it will become. It's a gift to yourself and your future you.

Your ICA isn't a fictional profile – it's a soul connection. When you know how they think, feel and act you don't need to 'market' to them; you just need to show up and speak to their desired future identity.

SEVEN
Meet My Ideal Client

In this chapter, I am going to show you what it looks like when you do the work on your ideal client. This is a real ICA I created using the exact process I have shared with you. Watch how the clarity around her personality builds as her story and connection to me unfold. Remember that this is just one of my ICAs; it doesn't mean I will only work with this exact person. I'm sharing it as an example for you to see how the process works. I'm opening up the co-creation space. Let's see what happens.

Let's create Emily

In Netflix Series 1 Episode 1, Emily is forty-six. She was a senior accountant until six years ago, when she hit forty and realised her whole life had been for other people. It was on a packed ferry in Greece, island-hopping as part of her 'Forty things to do in your forties' list she had written accompanied by '90s hip-hop and a bottle of Pinot Grigio a few weeks before. Jostling for space surrounded by suburban tourists with the sun on her face and the wind in her hair and thinking about going back to work the next week, she heard the whisper from her soul: 'That isn't your life; you are made for more.'

Of course, she went back to work, but it was like her eyes were now wide open in a world she had been sleepwalking in. Nothing made sense anymore: not the corner office, not the Hermès bag, not the clip-clop of her Manolo Blahniks, which scared the younger male staff members to death in the boardroom. The fourteen-hour days working for an organisation that cared only about money and winning made no sense. Emily realised that every qualification, every role, every promotion and pay rise had been to create a world that looked good from the outside, ticked every box, was the pinnacle of her parents' ambitions for her and sounded impressive at parties.

Born into a family of high achievers, Emily is the youngest of four, with three older brothers. Her childhood involved a lot of sport, wrestling, eating and taking the piss out of each other. It stood her in good stead when she was at school; any attempts to bully her were roundly dismissed, as she could belittle anyone with her words, and her lack of fear of physical fighting meant no one ever went near her, never mind the three older rugby-playing brothers in the years above. She used this position for good, splitting up fights quickly and stopping any bullying she saw by turning it round on the perpetrator but in good humour. Her teachers loved her because she was a perfectionist and an overachiever, often expanding on her homework with additional essays and being the first to step up to help with extracurricular activities. She went to a nice school in a nice area – not private, as there were four of them – but a good comprehensive near to the village where her dad was a GP and her mum was head teacher at the local primary school.

There was never a discussion about whether Emily wanted to go to uni – it was expected. Her brothers went off to study medicine, engineering and economics, and, because she loved numbers and being able to work out the answers to problems, Emily chose maths. She got a first because she was always first in everything – that's how she created self-worth and achieved recognition and made her parents proud when they talked about her in the village. She graduated and went to work as a junior accountant.

Through sheer hard work, bloody-mindedness and bold moves in a man's world, Emily became the youngest senior partner in a huge consulting firm at thirty-six. Aged forty, on that boat in Greece, she realised this achievement looked great from the outside but felt all kinds of wrong on the inside.

Some nights she came in late and poured the £14 Sauvignon before she took off her coat. Some nights she worked at her laptop until she fell asleep and woke up with it overheating in her bed at 6am, when she started working again. Some mornings she needed three double espressos to feel normal, and most evenings she spent with her husband staring past the TV into space and into the next day's work. Weekends were spent running her daughter around to her parties, scrolling, drinking and checking emails, worrying about real or imagined fires burning at work when she relaxed even for a minute.

Her husband, Dave, working in his big job in finance – Emily's not sure exactly what he does, Chandler Bing-style – was earning £230K plus bonuses and she was getting a package close to £150K. Their daughter, Isabella, was nearly five and starting school in her little straw hat and blazer that September and she had no idea how she was going to make any school events, never mind the school run. Isabella would be fine; she had been in wrap-around nursery care since she was six weeks old. The staff were often standing around or clearing chairs away while Isabella stood at the gate with her coat on waiting, like that last puppy at the pound.

It was time for action.

In the bravest, boldest move of her life, Emily handed in her notice and retrained as an executive coach. For the next five years, her life transformed in a way she hadn't thought was possible. Alongside doing some contract finance work, where she got to get dressed up and go into the city and throw a bit of that old weight around, she slowly but surely built a new business, getting clients through word of mouth and building a small but thriving practice. After the initial shock wore off, her family and partner and peers got behind the new venture, even throwing a little champagne party to launch it and sharing her posts on LinkedIn.

Fast-forward to now and the business is performing well on paper, albeit a mile away from replacing her salary. Emily is turning over £6K a month with one-to-one clients and topping that up with her consultancy work to make £10K a month. Good stuff, right? Ten thousand pounds a month, being her own boss and doing amazing, incredible, life-changing work with clients.

Except… the lovely Emily has swapped one job for another, one boss for a group of new bosses, and has precisely zero free time. She spends all day, every day in her office, working fourteen-hour days and dashing out to pick up Isabella from school, frazzled, then back to plonk her in front of the TV or the iPad while Emily gets back to client calls, emails, and sales and marketing activity. She has no freaking idea how to get clients online without it feeling like a fluke and lives in fear that all her clients will leave her and she will never get another one again.

The initial excitement and support from her husband, friends and family has long since fizzled out. No one likes or comments on her posts; they're more likely to take the mick out of her attempts at personal branding online. Her mum drops by most days and doesn't understand that she is working, Isabella is having more screen time than Emily would ever admit, and wine time is getting earlier and earlier. School runs are stressful and much less fun than she envisaged when she was staring out of her office window at 3pm.

She's bought a few courses and programmes and has taken something from them all – but that's the problem – she's ended up with a weak echo of their advice and a confusing daily routine of posting in random places and hoping for the best in between aimlessly scrolling and feeling furious at how everyone else is making it look effortless.

Emily is knackered and overwhelmed and is missing the scaffolding of having the big job: the marketing team, the admin team, the authority the name brought sitting there on her email footer and in her LinkedIn headline. Now she is feeling lost and lonely, having tried to 'find her community' like Instagram told her to, both online and offline. Online is chaotic and noisy, people are in cliques and endlessly falling out like children in a playground, and every time she thinks she's found her people it turns out it was money for not much. Online is a community that feels weird and people who are secretly and silently competing with her and hoping her successes don't outshine theirs. She thought she had left the politics behind, but they seem to have followed her. Which brings us to today.

The stick figure of Emily

My stick figure of Emily is surrounded by handwritten notes: 'Emily, forty-six, income £10K a month', 'Executive coach, workshops and one-to-one', 'Married to Dave, one daughter, Isabella, six', 'Lives in Hale, Dave earns £230K, house worth £900K, townhouse outside of town', 'They go to the country pub on Sunday, wine bar and gourmet Indian restaurant on date night', 'Brunch with mum friends on a Sunday because Dave plays golf on a Saturday and they swap childcare', 'Goes to the gym, eats pretty well, drinks more white wine than she would like', 'Loves scrolling socials, watching trash TV and is super spiritual', 'Into crystals, cards, manifesting and the Law of Attraction'.

Sad face

On my sad face of Emily before joining the programme, I write: 'Wants more money but not to work more hours – wants to be around people who get that', 'Hasn't found her place – feels lonely and disconnected', 'Has nowhere she can be honest about her struggles – has to be "always on" for clients and talking the talk with her family and friends', 'Tired. So tired. Feels emotionally, logistically, mentally and financially tired', 'Has clients that make her feel a kind of way that she doesn't like. Some are nice but boring; some are exciting but also late both in call attendance and invoice payment; some treat her like a friend and don't want to do the work', 'Frustrated with growth, scale and profitability', 'Social media posts not landing', 'Client acquisition is hit and miss', 'Referrals come but then feel diluted as clients refer clients who refer clients and they get further away from who she really wants to work with', 'Feels something is off, but isn't sure what', 'Feels like the business runs her, not the other way round', 'Struggles to know who to hire and for what but knows she needs help', 'Doesn't know what she needs to implement in terms of tech, funnels, software', 'Feels completely overwhelmed with social media and thinking she has to be present on them all, all of the time', 'Has dropped self-care, can't remember the last massage she had and is drinking too much. She's irritable, snappy and constantly on her phone. Says she's working but she is mainly scrolling', 'Is going to divorce Dave if he asks her even one more time when she's going to "get a proper job" or "consider going back to work"'.

Happy face

On the happy face of Emily after joining the programme, I write: 'Feels so much better. Lighter,

MEET MY IDEAL CLIENT

brighter, supported, happy. Like a new woman', 'Has put up her prices, dropped all red flag clients and feels great about it', 'Is connecting daily for three minutes and has so much more clarity, connection and inner peace', 'Loves her new clients and how they make her feel, totally different vibe', 'Feels good getting up and content going to sleep', 'Goes to the Facebook group most days and has built some really strong friendships including meeting up for lunch outside of the programme', 'Is a much nicer partner, parent and person. Says hello to everyone on the street and is extra nice to waitresses. Is a big tipper', 'Has complete clarity on who she is talking to when she puts pen to paper, thumb to phone or fingers to keyboard. Her content zings off the page, she gets loads of positive feedback and it converts into sales. She feels like she has magical powers', 'Making more money, is having more fun, is making more impact', 'Thinks bigger and bolder every day', 'Has embraced spirituality in a much deeper way and is integrating it into everything she is doing both in life and business', 'Has found so many brilliant experts and specialists to help her in all aspects of her business and life, all through the community'.

Dave is happy, let's just say that. Underneath the faces I make other notes about how my offer helps Emily.

What does Emily love about the group programme?

'Loves the Facebook community – is the first place she goes every day and when she has a question or needs to share a win or a wobble. It makes her feel safe, seen and supported as well as part of a gang. For someone who often felt the odd one out, it feels like a place she can fit in. She gives as much as she gets and is part of the family.'

'Loves the portal – the step by step is right up her street, stops her getting overwhelmed and means she can go back if needed and also forwards if she's in the zone. Really enjoys the video content and has watched hours of me to the point I can answer her questions in her head energetically.'

'Loves the calls – the high-achieving part of her enjoys showing up every week, notepad and pen in hand, and getting an injection of motivation and support and feeling part of something live and in the moment.'

'Loves how it is structured – "There is no behind" is the mantra, and she really appreciates that feeling of running her own race, at her own pace, and how no matter what life throws at her the programme is there for her when she is ready.'

'Loves the lifetime access – it really makes her feel this was a worthwhile investment as she grows and changes, the programme is always there to support her. No feeling under pressure to get a result in six weeks or even six months. Loves that some people have been there for a decade.'

'Loves the vibe – positive, action-focused with a massive spirituality element, which makes her feel like she's totally in the right place.'

'Loves the team and the support coaches and experts – feels like she gets more support, more expertise and more ways to move herself forwards.'

'Loves that it's all online – can log in from anywhere and means she can travel, work away and prioritise family when needed.'

What does she love about me?

'Straight-talking, no-nonsense, direct and northern', 'Super spiritual but also super strategic – hasn't met anyone who has that balance', 'Been there, done that – I've done so many things she wants to do and yet seem just like her', 'Parent like she is, gets the juggle', 'Swears, drinks, is "unprofessional" and loves having a laugh and a good time, like her', 'Generous with time, energy and advice yet has boundaries where necessary, which is how she wants to show up', 'Big-hearted and kind – loves the charity work side and the pay-it-forward vibe', 'Doesn't need or want everyone to like them – which, as a people pleaser, she finds magnetic', 'Animal lover – she loves the pics of Dave the sausage dog and the cats, Tina and Terry', 'Into health and fitness to a point – like her'.

IDEAL CLIENT ATTRACTION

Why is now the time for Emily to take action?

It's time to join the group programme because if she stays where she is things will get worse, not better. There's also a launch period open right now which closes soon and she wants the bonuses.

What next?

To join, all she needs to do is click the link or book a call. Or send a DM.

I hope this explains how I do my own ICA work. I have different ICAs for all my products and services and often revisit, refine and redo my ICA maps. I use the pin-the-tail-on-the-donkey method of closing my eyes and picking anything off the map to create a jumping-off point for content. I also feed my maps into ChatGPT to create a much more aligned output.

> **YOUR TURN**
>
> Write a fresh ICA map for your offer. Try to dig into the things the avatar is not saying. Go deep, have fun, fall in love with the process. Handwrite your notes to feel even more connected and put them up where you can see them.

MEET MY IDEAL CLIENT

This chapter has illustrated how everything changes when you fully see your ideal client. You stop creating generic content. You stop doubting your value. You start speaking straight to the soul of the person you are here to serve – and they feel it. This isn't just a marketing tool – it's a sacred alignment practice.

EIGHT

Attract And Magnetise Your Ideal Client

This is where we bring it all together and start taking action and getting results. Attraction isn't about shouting louder – it's about tuning your energy so clearly that the right clients can't miss you. In this chapter we move from knowing your ICA to becoming magnetic to them – consistently, intentionally and without chasing. Now we know *who* we want to attract, it's about *where* and *how* we get in front of them and help them to see and feel safe that we are the person to help them solve their problems.

If my work is truly manifestation in action, then this is where we meet the universe halfway. We have set our intention, got into the energy of achieving our goal of magnetising those ideal clients, raised our vibration by being amazing and spent time in daily devotion to attracting those perfect people to us. The universe will be conspiring to bring us together to make real this vision as a co-creation, but we have to do our part of taking inspired action every day towards our desire and being open to all aligned opportunities that come our way. We have to move, not sit and wait.

EXERCISE: The daily three-minute client connection practice

This brings together the three one-minute practices, so you have a way to check in and connect every day – any place, anywhere.

Go quiet. Take a couple of long, deep breaths. Drop from your head energy into your heart energy and breathe into that. Let your body sink a little.

Connect to yourself – how are you feeling today, what do you need today?

Connect to your offer – how does it feel today, what does it need today?

Connect to your client – how do they feel today, what do they need to hear from you today?

Spend a little time seeing what comes up.

From that energetic connective energy take action. Write the post, send the email, step onto that stage, press that Go Live button.

Everything will change.

Growth = engagement = sales

Daily visibility matters, energetically and strategically. Marketing is about getting attention in an increasingly busy world. In all the years I have been simultaneously doing it for myself and teaching it as I go, it's not changed much.

There's an old fable I shall clumsily paraphrase. There was a deeply religious man stranded on a desert island. A storm came and the raging water was rising minute by minute. 'God, please save me,' he shouted into the wind. Along came a fishing boat. 'Get in!' the fisherman shouted from close to shore. 'No. God will save me,' the man shouted back. The man drowned and arrived in heaven with God. 'Why didn't you save me?' he asked. 'I sent the boat,' said God.

Look for the boats, and jump in when you get the chance. Start building your own boats every day while you wait.

Business success comes down to growing your audience, engaging with your audience and selling to your audience. It's simple and I think we make it super complicated. I'm a fan of making things as easy and fun as possible. If every day you think, *How can I leverage my time, energy and resources today to grow, engage and convert my audience?*, you will have a head start on most people I meet in this context, who are sitting around worrying about what to say, what to post and when and where, or doing another certification or twiddling with their branding or websites.

The sooner you get comfortable outside your comfort zone, the sooner you will see real growth. The more you do what feels safe and easy, the more you stay in your whirlpool of people who know you. The more you keep hanging out where you're already known, the harder exponential growth becomes. Walking into a room where everyone knows you is hanging out with your mates; walking into a room where no one knows you is marketing. It's the same online. Same old communities, same old groups, same old leads and sales versus new places, new people, new leads, new opportunities, new growth.

The rings in your social media audience

In your social media audience there are a number of layers.

The ride or dies: These are the soul-aligned people who like you, love you, want more of you: your super fans. They rave about you in rooms you are not in. You can post almost anything as a half-formed offer and they will buy it. They invest in you because it's you. They want to be as close to you as possible; they love your energy, your insights and your vibe. They are your biggest fans, and they will take your business a long way. Nurture these people and they will be a huge part of your success story. I love these guys. I can post 'I am thinking about doing a thing...' and they are straight in my DMs wanting it, without even knowing what it is. You can get (dangerously) complacent if you sit back and relax and think you've cracked it.

The paying clients: They have bought from you before, they love and respect your work, they value and respect your time and expertise. They are in your world because they want to be in your energy and you have a positive mutually beneficial relationship. They buy from you the things they need and they will buy again if the timing and the offer are right. A rich source of revenue, love and support, these people make your time online a positive one.

The cheerleaders: They are in your orbit because they get something positive from you and they reciprocate by supporting you, commenting on your stuff, sharing your posts and generally bigging you up even when you're not in the room. They're not in a position to buy – maybe they need more money, maybe it's not the right time, or maybe they'll never need what you sell but they love you and support you anyway. Your mum probably falls into the latter category, as do old friends and acquaintances that haven't got sick of your posts about your business and love to keep up with what you are doing. Never underestimate the power of these people. They can make your social media world rich, varied and fun to be in.

The stumblers: They don't know how they stumbled across you and they don't know how you ended up in their feed, but there you are. They can be brought closer to you, but you need to be explicit in who you help, how you help and what you charge to do so. They need to be entertained, educated and mesmerised to turn them from a stumbler to a cheerleader to a paying client and through to the ride-or-die ring.

Create content for every ring and you won't go too far wrong; just create for one and you may hit a results plateau sooner rather than later.

If you meet me in real life, there is a high chance I will ask you an annoying question: 'Have you posted your offer today?' You will most likely say no, or not yet, probably because we are at an event and you're busy, so think you didn't have time to post, or you haven't posted it today, because you posted it yesterday and you don't want people to think you're too salesy, or desperate, or annoying.

It's interesting how the biggest brands in the world, the household names like McDonald's, Coca-Cola and Apple, don't worry about such things and are advertising in a million places and spaces all over the world every single day – a clue to how they became the biggest brands in the world. I was fascinated to see Amazon heavily promoting in the week before Christmas in the UK; I thought it was interesting that in their busiest period as *the* go-to for Christmas shopping online, they were pushing hard for more. There's you thinking people will judge you for putting an offer out twice in a day. No one cares if you're selling every day, and if they do, they're not your ideal client. Paying your bills and looking after your family matter, what other people think of your sales strategies doesn't.

I get it, though. It's knowing where to show up and what to say and how to post. I know this is a massive block, because I have heard it a million times, but I feel this is pressure you don't need to put on yourself. Permission to drop it granted.

Instead of trying to become a marketing strategist or learning to be a copywriter, what if you could just show up as you and that be compelling enough? What if the secret is that what the world needs is more people being more themselves and fewer trying to fit into what other people are telling them to be?

All strategies and tactics work

Whether it's sending endless DMs on LinkedIn, knocking door to door or creating intricate automated sales funnels, they all work; it is more about how they make you feel and how they impact your energy. If you are using a tactic you hate and that makes you feel weird and rejected and frustrated, then it's not going to feel good and you're not going to sustain it long term even if it is working. Some might love the challenge of cold-calling and see it as a game they love to win; others would rather die than risk being told to get lost by a stranger. Some people love the geekiness of the creative/data mix of the funnel; others love the human energetics of the in-person sale. They all work. All platforms work.

Some platforms feel like home and some feel like an unfamiliar land. Trust yourself and double down on the ones you love and leave the ones that make you feel you're on Planet Zog. Can you learn to love any platform, any strategy, any tactic? Yes, to a point. I used to meet a *lot* of resistance to LinkedIn when I focused on LinkedIn strategy as my main offer. I used to roll my digital eyes when I would see a post about how people hate it on Facebook over and over again. I would try to not roll my actual eyes when I would meet someone at an event and they would say 'Oh, you're the LinkedIn woman, I hate LinkedIn.' I would reply 'Would you hate it if you made £100K a year on there?' and they would say 'I'd love it', then I would spend time trying to show them how amazing the platform is and where the opportunity was.

I realised I could focus my time on people who *wanted* to embrace LinkedIn, were sure that was where their clients were and just wanted someone to show them what to do; that was a much easier life for me. I used to think everyone should be on LinkedIn because there is so much money to be made and it's so easy to use, but then I realised how I feel about Instagram: I get it, I see the potential, I just don't feel at home there. I could invest a lot of time and energy into it and it would definitely pay off, but I can also hang out on Facebook (my spiritual home and number-one place to hang out) and LinkedIn and have a nice life too. Choosing where you're happiest and making that work is the path of least resistance, and I am all about that life now.

All strategies work – if you enjoy working them – because if you find a strategy you love, you will show up consistently and be prepared to try things and fail and try things and fly, because it feels good anyway.

No strategies work as well as they could, however, if you don't know who your ideal client is. The good news is that you are reading this book and we have got this covered. Now you know your ICA by name, know what their problems are, the outcomes you deliver and what they value about your offer and you, *all* your strategies are going to work better. Wahoo!

Everything you write, everything you post, every video you make, every email you send, every sales page you create, every funnel you build, every advert you make and every talk you deliver is now designed with one person in mind: your ideal client. Before you put thumb to phone or pen to paper, open Zoom, step onto the stage, walk into that meeting, you're going to think one thing and one thing only: *What does [Insert ICA name] need to hear from me today?*

When you have got your plan and settled on your platforms and tactics, then it's time to start showing up in this shiny new energy – you have the tools to connect to it.

Whatever you do strategically above the line has an impact, or an echo or a reflection, below the line. Showing up and posting on social media may make you feel vulnerable or anxious. Getting no comments might make you feel rejected and humiliated. Sending out an email that gets a ton of sign-ups might make you feel excited and positive. Getting on a sales call might make you feel nervous and excited all at once – or not. These are just examples of how everything we do in business and everything that happens in our business has an impact on how we think and feel. How we think and feel has an impact on everything we do in our business, which impacts everything that happens in our business.

How can we stop our emotions impacting our energy and our energy impacting our actions? It's all about self-awareness. It's knowing when you are in your bottom-left quadrant and feeling all the feelings and moving yourself across before you take action.

Turn whining energy into winning energy

There are generally two energies that prompt social media posts: whining energy and winning energy.

Whining energy fuels those posts you see that are born out of anger, frustration, a sense of injustice, defensiveness, despair. They are usually moaning about something that's happened or is happening in their business, like being copied or clients wanting refunds, or it's a passive-aggressive, naming-no-names post about someone who has upset them. Sometimes it's bad-mouthing other competitors or other tactics that don't align with them; often it's about a lack of authenticity and integrity around them. It's all coming from a place of fear, anger or hurt. These posts attract a lot of attention and conflict or a deluge of support and soothing from people who feel the same. These people do not look like they are having a good time. It's one way to show up on social media, just not one I would recommend. It will get you clients and money but it also attracts people who are drawn to that energy and are going to create more of that energy in your business.

Winning energy fuels those posts you see that are born out of excitement, joy and pride and a sense of enthusiasm, happiness and positivity. They are usually ideas, concepts and insights shared to help others or funny, interesting or unusual posts to entertain. They are posted in great energy, full of passion and power, and are compelling to read. They make people feel inspired and enthused with the energy and come from a place of high vibration that can be felt. These people look like they are having a great time whether you buy from them or not. I would highly recommend *only* posting when you are in winning energy.

You know when you are in whining energy, because you are deep in your soul-negative quadrant. You are feeling the feelings and it is not good. You are thinking negative thoughts and your energy is low. It could be that you are tired, something has happened, someone has said something, you've seen or heard something that's triggered you, or it could just be one of those days. This is perfectly normal, but stop and breathe and think before you take that energy and go public with it. Alchemise it with your actions first. Go for a walk, take a nap, have a snack, drink some water, vent to a trusted friend, scream into a pillow, have a good cry, stroke a pet, watch funny videos, belt out your favourite song, do some star jumps. Go to your testimonials folder on your phone and read the kind words your clients say. Look at your notes from the ICA map and remember who you're here to help. Remind yourself of the impact you are here to have. Only then are you ready to post.

You know when you are in winning energy because you can feel it. A client raves about you, you make a sale, you come off a call, your launch goes brilliantly, you step off stage – you are on top of your game and feeling amazing and *that* is the energy to post from. Go, go, go and don't stop. When you are in the zone and feeling great, post as much as you want and as often as you want. When your energy is good and your creative juices are flowing and it feels like you have so much to say and so much to share, say it and share it – don't let the fear of sharing or saying too much ever hold you back. Don't schedule it – share it in the energy of the moment because people will feel the energy through your posts. Schedulers are where post energy goes to die – don't kill it, set it free. Don't worry about the algorithm or what people might think if you post a lot, because what you have to say is important to you to say, so say it. It will reach the right people, don't worry.

Showing up and sharing who you are, what you are here to do, what you want to say and how you want to make a difference in the world is the secret of social media. It's back to how it was before marketers ruined it and started creating all these rules. Growing your audience by adding new people to it every day, through asking to connect or showing up and engaging publicly so people can find their own way to you, will ensure new people are seeing your stuff. Without the growth, you will be talking to the same people and will see results in terms of sales start to plateau quickly, as everyone who was going to buy still buys from you and the rest are just watching and waiting for the timing to be right, or they're never going to buy – all equally fine, it's just you need a growing audience if you are to grow your business online.

Simple and free audience growth

A simple and free way to grow your audience is being a guest expert. You can do this by delivering training in someone else's community, or you can be a guest on someone else's podcast. When you start out you will probably be doing training in small communities and being a guest on small podcasts, and that's to be expected – just make sure you show up like there are a million people watching and listening, and someday there will be.

Another good way is to choose two or three Facebook groups where your ideal client hangs out and immerse yourself in them. I mean truly immerse yourself in the community, not attempt a smash and grab. Understand the group and the intention of the group owner and invest time and energy every day in helping that group and supporting its members in a neutral way. Over time, you will become known and people will seek you out and join your audience.

Press, PR and public speaking are all ways to get in front of new people. Pitching yourself to local and national publications, making sure you 'create a story' for the audience, will bring new people to you.

If you have money to invest, paid advertising can be a wonderful way to get people into your world by hardly lifting a finger; however, I would wait until you are confident you have a rock-solid offer, conversion mechanism (a webinar, challenge, scorecard, sales call etc) and sales process before you start, and I would always advise consulting with an expert.

You are growing your audience and showing up and shining as the wonderful human you are, using your map and your practice to inspire you every day on what to write to speak to your ICA on a deep level by making them feel your content is written just for them – because it is. This certainly gets their attention, but how do you convert them from curiously educated and entertained into taking those all-important steps towards you?

You present your offer to them in a way that speaks to their soul.

Yes, you have to tick every logical box. Talk to tangible outcomes, talk to certain results, talk about the transformation you are confident you can provide. Give them what they want but tell them what they need. They need to know you are to be trusted. They need to feel safe with you. They need to feel you are 100% confident you can help them. Certainty sells. You have to be certain you can help them, just as they have to be certain you're the person to help them. Entrusting you with their time, energy and money requires a certain level of vulnerability that needs to be acknowledged, respected and cared for. Even when 'selling to corporates', this is possibly even more important. People who work in big organisations are people too. They have hopes and dreams, highs and lows, wins and losses just like everyone else. You are never selling to the organisation, always to the person who makes the decision. You map them exactly the same, except this time you are going to take the money and they are going to take the credit. You have to get them to trust you so they come to your side of the table and you build a business case together. You are going to make them feel a million dollars walking into that boardroom having fixed the problem. They will take the accolades and the pay rise and the authority of success and you will be their secret weapon.

Talk to them on a human level, on an in-the-darkness-at-4am level. That sounded more creepy predator than I intended; I mean the waking-up-and-unable-to-get-back-to-sleep-inside-thoughts level, the anxiety, hopes, dreams and regret level – not standing by the end of their bed. Talk about the things they are not talking about, about the things they are thinking and feeling more than the things that everyone knows are happening because they can see. The things they are afraid to even say out loud.

Take an HR director for example. Brenda is fifty-one and has been in HR for a whole lot of years. She worked her way up from her graduate scheme to where she is now. She is both exhausted and frustrated. Everyone can see recruitment is a problem, absenteeism is on the rise, presenteeism, even though it is a term coined only a few years back, is on the rise. In her day it was called 'taking the piss' and don't get her started on 'quiet quitting'. Brenda is fully aware there is a problem, but she doesn't need that pointing out because that's what the seventy-two emails a day she gets from wellbeing service providers say. Brenda is tired. Tired of the endless interruptions on her working day. Tired of the other directors speaking over her in meetings because she's a woman. Tired of hearing about the strategic 'breakthroughs' made by the pale, male, stale leadership team on the golf course and during the nine pints and a curry after. She's sick of looking at her Spreadsheet of Doom, where all the stats are going in the wrong direction. Good people are leaving, she is always firefighting, no one is listening to her and she goes home and takes it out on Derek, her lovely but useless fifty-eight-year-old husband she met thirty-five years ago when they were both more enthusiastic about life and less wide around the middle. She looks at Derek telling her about his day in engineering when she comes back from work, but she's barely listening; she's thinking about opening the wine before she gets her coat off. She can't remember the last time she did anything fun.

IDEAL CLIENT ATTRACTION

Brenda opens up her laptop at 9pm after dinner with a long, loud sigh. She sees your post, it makes sense. It talks to her soul. It says 'You're in HR and you don't need me to tell you you need help but guess what I can do... I can actually improve wellbeing (and prove it), keep people happy and keep them away from your office door for only £5K and *one* single meeting.' Now she's interested.

It's as simple as that. Talk about problems and solutions in a simple way like you would speak in your normal voice. For example, think about working with your ideal client and consider the following:

- How does their life change?
- How do they feel when you have worked together?
- What's the ripple effect?
- How does their success make you feel?

With Brenda you come in, have a meeting, deliver a wellbeing strategy and everyone is happier and more content and chills out and stops creating drama for Brenda. You've had your £5K and worked a day and only need to do one a week for your £20K target, so you're happy.

For Brenda everything changes. She can get her work done. The stats start looking good. The Spreadsheet of Doom has a whole different file name now. The directors can't argue with the impact. They start to take her seriously. She feels bolder and re-energised now she has time and space to think. She considers leaving the company and also leaving Derek. She decides to go for a new job, taking you with her as her secret weapon. She talks about the impact her initiative had at the company. The new people ooh and aah at the spreadsheet results. They want the same. Brenda gets a £10K pay rise and a Tesla and you get another £5K as soon as she has sign-off. Derek lives to fight another day.

> **YOUR TURN**
>
> Write your ICA map from start to finish and commit to a minimum of three audience growth strategies to get in front of them. Commit to being consistent in your posting, engaging and selling.

Magnetising your ideal client doesn't require more time, more content or more tactics. It requires alignment. When you show up every day in BCE and are clear, connected and consistent, your ideal client will feel it. When they feel it, they follow.

NINE

When The Going Gets Tough

Even when you're in alignment, things can wobble. Engagement dips. Fear creeps in. Visibility feels vulnerable. We've talked about where and why and how to show up, but what about when you don't feel like it? What about when life gets in the way? What about when bad things happen, or even good things that take you away from your business and into a different world? In this chapter, we'll talk about what to do when the work gets uncomfortable and how to show up with power and purpose when your ego wants to hide.

You need to show up even when you don't feel like it. I would say this has been my superpower over the many years I've worked online. My friends used to say 'How can you go from crying on the phone to me about something and then five minutes later you're on a live saying "Hi, welcome to..."?'

I don't let my emotions dictate my activity. I show up for my business like I am getting paid a million dollars no matter what. Many times I have done live training to no viewers, been the guest expert where no one shows up and been on podcasts that no one listens to – but I show up the same regardless. I post almost every day and some posts get traction and others don't and sometimes I post offers that no one buys and sometimes they fly. I show up the same regardless. I put myself out there and people don't like me and I show up the same regardless. I am committed to my business on every level – strategically, emotionally, spiritually – because no matter how I feel, there is someone out there who needs to hear what I have got to say. I am in service. It's a bit like going to the gym. You don't expect to get new muscles every time you go. You understand that it's a process and a case of showing up, putting in the reps and being consistent. I skip the gym sometimes because I don't mind being a little out of shape, but I am consistent in my business because I do mind being broke.

Become unstoppable

What can you do to commit to your business and commit to serving your client so nothing can put you off-track?

I see so many people become despondent when they don't get the results they want or expect instead of addressing the one thing they can control: their dedication to showing up for their business regardless. They decide the strategy or tactics don't work and start a brand-new one where they don't get instant results either. Put yourself in your ICA's shoes. They are noticing and watching and sensibly wanting to make sure you are committed to showing up before they reach out and invest... and then you disappear to try something else or go somewhere else or start selling something else and all that time was wasted.

Getting into alignment with who you are, what you are offering and who it is for is of course the important part; then it is about getting famous for your thing in your niche by being consistent and building your authority and reputation. Bad news if you were looking for the quick fix, I know, but I am here to give you the truth. Consistency wins and the sooner you start, the sooner you will start to build something that no one else can compete with you on: time.

When I started out as 'the LinkedIn person' I did three sessions for free to test my concept of teaching people my methods in one hour. Then I charged £99 per session and that was my offer. Same offer, same graphic, same social media platforms and groups. I showed up all day, every day, in multiple ways. I was posting my own content, doing Facebook lives every day (in those days to my mum, mainly, still my number-one fan – love you, Mum), engaging on other people's posts, contributing to groups and posting on LinkedIn every day. I was pitching for guest expert opportunities every day (and mainly getting ignored) with people who had communities and speaking day and night as a guest expert for the kind people who gave me a chance (thank you, Dan Meredith, for my first one), plus running my sessions day and night round the girls. It's a graft, it's about being time-served, about your name getting known. Only then did I launch a group programme and then consistently launch it six times a year for many years. There were no shortcuts but there were quantum leaps as the consistency, authority and audience growth strategies started to pay off. It's definitely not about one secret hack or sitting on the beach with your laptop or having six weeks off with your children in the summer.

The lifestyle comes later. It did for me. Five years later I had made millions from my group programme and was being asked to go on podcasts, being paid to be a guest expert and speaking on stages all over the world. I am now known as the 'ideal client person', but that is after ten years of consistency and a conscious decision to focus on exactly what you are reading now. I will be teaching this for the next decade. I still do guest expert talks, go on podcasts and post all the time, because those methods work and work forever no matter what happens next. I do it because I know there's someone out there who needs to hear what I have got to say. That's what drives me every day even if I'm not feeling it.

Be yourself – it's the best marketing hack

The more 'you' you can be, the more your ideal client will be magnetised towards you. Realness is intoxicating and mesmerising in a world of smoke and mirrors, fakery and deception and marketing manipulation. Having a clear channel between the real you and your ideal client is like a hotline to their soul, and it works both ways. How can you expect them to feel safe with you if you aren't prepared to be open and honest and vulnerable with them?

Now, don't get this wrong. I do not mean documenting every awful thing that happens to you as it happens. I mean talking honestly about who you are and what made you that way. I don't mean drama, emotions and chaos as a content pillar. I mean thinking about how people bond – it's by sharing secrets and showing what's underneath the you that everyone gets to see. People buy from people who have their shit together with the thing that they sell, but they are fascinated and relieved when they realise you don't have *all* your shit together, all the time. In my experience, anyway. People often say to me 'Oh, you're so normal' when they meet me. I don't know how to be any other way than the way that I am. OK, I will be 10% more sparkly and sparky when I am online delivering training or promoting something and maybe 10% less when I am picking up dog poo or doing the dishwasher, but basically what you see is what you get.

I remember when I hit £1 million revenue for the first time. I was sitting in my little front office running the numbers in Xero and making notes on my paper and the figure was something like £1,100,324.56. I sat and looked at it. Nothing happened. No confetti fell from the ceiling, no marching band appeared, nothing. My hair did not get bouncy like it did for all the other seven-figure course creators I had seen. I had cat hair on my hoodie and an unidentified small stain. I stood up, pushed my chair back and went to the kitchen. The cat was exactly where I had left her. I fed her, did the dishwasher, went for a walk. As I walked around in my shit coat and dirty trainers, I thought, *No one looking at me would think I made a million* and *I bet all the seven-figure podcast people will want me on now*, and then I went home and back to work. It was only posting about it on socials that made it feel real, and everyone was so happy for me and then it felt even more real. (Well, obviously not everyone, but I let them watch and be furious and say things like 'Yeah, but how much is profit?', 'Turnover is vanity, profit is sanity' and 'How much on ads though?', yadda yadda yadda – all the things that people say when they can't just say 'Wow, well done, you made a million pounds appear out of nowhere with your hard work – well done you'.) Hitting a goal you've had for a long time is so weird; you don't know how to react. I didn't, anyway.

The thing with trying to be someone you are not is that it is bloody hard work. I think this is part of the corporate burnout problem: loads of lovely humans trying to contort themselves into who the organisation needs them to be. Trying to be perfect online will fry your brain and confuse your audience. Be fantastic at the thing you sell, yes, but unless you're fantastic at everything, including being a human being, relax.

I am on a mission for radical honesty in our marketing. Being clear on who you help, how you help and how much you charge is going to make everyone's lives easier. People are busy and the world is noisy. I write all my own posts except for promotional ones in the run-up to a launch or an event, because I haven't got enough fingers and toes with the amount of posts we put out. I sort of write my emails: they are my thoughts and words given to an expert email writer. I wouldn't know how to work our email software. I would definitely break it and send the wrong thing to nearly a hundred thousand people.

My social media posts are me, though, and I think that is important from both sides. There is almost zero friction between me thinking about something and sharing it. If it pops into my head, I share it. I never sit down to write content at my computer – it is always on my phone, in the moment. I don't use notes, I don't save ideas for later, I definitely don't use schedulers. I want to share it in the energy I am feeling it, whether it's an insight or a cat video. Most of my posts are written after I have done something to give me head space. I'm usually sitting in a towel dripping water all over the screen after a shower or sitting on the sofa next to the cage at kickboxing after a session or sitting on my drive in the car after coming in from a trip out. I post anywhere, anytime. If I have three things to say, I will say them, all one after the other. I post daytime, night-time and at weekends. I post at 4am if I am awake. I don't give a shit about the 'algorithm' and I never have – and I have done OK. Imagine worrying about what time to post, or how long a post should be, or if you should use an image or a link, or if you can use the word 'free' without spelling it 'fr33', or how long a video should be, or how many times you can post, or what keywords to use and on and on and on. Exhausting. Post what you want when you want and as much as you want in the way that you want. How about that as a content strategy?

My four pillars of content

I talk about four pillars of content:

1. Telling stories
2. Posting video

3. Sharing social proof

4. Putting out offers

These are to remind you that people want to get to know you and how they can buy. Looking to me or anyone else to tell you exactly what to post and when just tells you that you are not to be trusted, that you can't decide what to say when and how and where, and you can. You already know what you want to say and where you want to say it. It's inside you, not inside this book. Go inwards and ask yourself, 'What do I want to share today? How do I want to show up today? Where do I need to be today?' Be led by what feels good and fun and easy. Don't force yourself into strategies because someone else says they are the answer. You already know the answer.

You will get real miserable, real fast if you force yourself into doing things that don't align. When you start something new, like doing videos, you will know the difference between 'This feels a bit awkward and weird but I am excited to see how it goes' and 'This feels hard and horrible and I will do anything to avoid doing it and it feels like a punishment every day'. I have to hold my hand up and say an earlier, less evolved, version of me was very much about doing things that felt hard no matter what, but I was doing myself and my audience a disservice there. Today, I do things that feel fun and easy for me on a soul level (even if some days it feels hard to get going), and you should do the same. This is a long-ass game if you want to play it full out, so find ways to show up that you enjoy and then overlay the discipline on the tough days.

The minimum viable product

About the tough days. Don't think I don't have them. Over my online career I have had some things happen behind the scenes that nearly broke me. I've had traumatic things happen at home and a whole load of things happen behind the scenes of my business. Maybe one day I'll write a book about these, but I would have to write it as fiction, as no one would believe me. I've also had many, many common or garden bad days where bad things happen and they would be the perfect excuse for not showing up in my business.

What do I do? I call it the minimum viable product. What's the minimum I need to put out to keep visible and keep selling? It could be a one-line post, sharing a funny video or posting an image that has my offer on; it could be commenting on a few posts or posting in my groups. It is not the day for writing intense long-form copy, being creative or hilarious or launching anything new. Slow and steady, but something goes out. A lot of my content is 'average at best'. I don't feel the pressure to write insightful content all the time or stick to a schedule (ugh) or write high-converting sales copy or anything like that. Sometimes I write a post and I think, *That is a banger* and I know it is going to go well with lots of engagement and it does, but most of the time I don't get many comments, because that's not the game I am playing. The game I am playing is showing up consistently, caring deeply about my ideal client and creating an environment where they can get to know me and I can help them. If I was playing the engagement game, I would post controversial posts about the industry or videos of me crying or polarising content about politics or current affairs of the day. Engagement is easy to get if that's the game you want to play, and no judgement from me: you do you.

Detach from the outcome

The one thing I do and I suggest you do is post it and forget it. It's done. What happens with it and to it is out of your hands. Don't worry about it; you've got more posts to do and more things to say – focus on those. Obsessing over reach or engagement or any other metric isn't going to change them. Yes, you can become a data scientist and test and measure and look for trends if you want, but I wouldn't if I were you.

One especially important media here is video. The only way to get good at video is to do more videos, so your early ones aren't going to be great. My top tips for video are:

- Never watch it back.
- Never ask for feedback.

There's nothing worse than watching and listening to yourself. Just let it go. It is done. I get unsolicited feedback on my videos *all* the time. You talk too fast, you talk too loudly, you talk too quietly, you swear too much, you're too northern, you move around in your chair too much, you wave your hands about too much, you go off on tangents too much, you drink too much, you get distracted by your kids too much and on and on and on. It is just how I talk and how I show up. Imagine if I tried to change to suit everyone who has an opinion on me.

I've done thousands of hours of video, including live video, and nothing fazes me anymore. I've had power cuts, people bursting in, friends knocking and waving at the window, the cat bringing a live mouse in, the cat pulling down the Christmas tree, a whole bath of water coming through the ceiling, people falling down the stairs, and one time my daughter stood on a bumblebee and got stung. I have coughed, spluttered, sneezed, spilt drinks, exploded champagne all over the place, had a panic attack and been a bit sick in my mouth. What can I say? It's showbiz and the show must go on.

What I want to portray to anyone watching is that I am a normal person who wants them to win. What your audience wants is to feel your confidence and certainty that you can help them. This is why I asked in Chapter Four about you being certain you can deliver the outcome you promise. It's difficult if that isn't there. I urge you to make your promise small and certain, because this will underpin everything you say and do in your business. Extreme confidence in results is compelling. Selling something huge that you are not quite certain you can deliver is a recipe for misalignment, doubt and hesitation, which will scare your potential clients away. Clients can sense it, even if you think you are doing a good job of hiding it. Go in and search for that one thing you can help your clients with. All the other things you can do and will do will be the icing on the cake, the drawing back of the curtain, the wow and the wonder, the over-delivery that will turn them into raving fans. Get them on the simple promise and blow their socks off with the rest.

One of the biggest hesitations I hear is 'What will people think?' The impact of worrying about other people's opinions is not to be underestimated. If I could wave a magic wand and get you to stop worrying about what other people might think or might say or might do, I absolutely would. People will think, say and do whatever they want to. You can't control that any more than a random person out there can control what you think, say or do. Hell, we can barely control our own thoughts, feelings and actions some days, so why would we even waste a minute thinking about what other people are doing? I know people have thought, felt and done negative things because of how I show up, because they tell me. They tell me I am too much, that I scared them, that they didn't like what I had to say, that I was too direct, that my posts were too many so they blocked me, that they unsubscribed from my emails because they were too salesy, that they left my group because they didn't like the way I replied to them... and so on and so forth. Even people who now love me tell me that they didn't like me when they first met me.

You know what? There's nothing I could have done about it, and that's OK. I was just showing up as me, good old imperfect me. I am sometimes rude or annoying or too much for some people. I am not for them and that's OK. I allow people to Goldilocks me for themselves. For some I am too much, for others not enough and for some just right. I don't try to convince the too-much people that I can be less, just for them, or the not-enough people that I can be more, just for them. Instead, I love my just-enough people hard, because they are my people. This is the way of peace and happiness and, luckily enough, success. For some people you will be too much. For some people you will be not enough. For some people you, the imperfect, messy human that you are, showing up with a good heart to do good work will be just right.

I am just right for you, because you have read this far. You are just right for me, because you have read this far. We have found each other and that is all that matters. I believe in you and your ability to commit to your business and show up in this absurd world like the perfect human that you are day after day, week after week, year after year and create something beyond your wildest dreams. Stop wanting 'just enough' and start expecting miracles.

> **YOUR TURN**
>
> Show up for yourself and your business every day like your dream life depends on it, because it does.

It's normal to second-guess yourself and wonder if your strategy is working, but what makes you magnetic isn't perfection – it's consistency. It's showing up anyway. This chapter is your permission slip to be human… and your invitation to stay in the room when most people leave.

We're in this together. Let's make business feel good again. I believe in you. You've got this. Let's go.

Conclusion: The Revolution Starts With You

You've done something powerful by getting to the end of this book – you've chosen to lead with alignment, soul and intention. That alone sets you apart from the noise of the online world, but this is just the beginning.

Within the pages of this book we have explored some key themes around clarity, connection and transformation, and you now have an offer you feel aligned with, an offer the client wants to buy and an ICA for that offer.

You know exactly where your ideal client is and where they will be in the future after working with you. You know exactly what attracts them to you and what they value most about you and your offer.

You have a simple spiritual and strategic practice to do each day to infuse your content, videos, emails, talks, sales calls and more with your ideal client's words, thoughts, feelings and energy to attract them directly to you. Ideal-client-infused content activates your ideal client towards you ready and excited to work with you. You don't need to overcome objections, they just need to know the next step.

Now you get to decide: will this stay as inspiration on the page, or will you take it into the world and make magic happen?

Your ideal clients are waiting. Not for a new sales funnel. Not for a shinier strategy. They're waiting for the most fully aligned version of *you* – visible, clear and magnetic as hell.

Next steps

If you're ready to go deeper with this work, I invite you into my group programme It's where we take everything in this book and put it into simple, soulful, strategic action – together. For regular wisdom, tough love and practical client attraction content, follow and engage with me on Facebook.

The group programme community is your space to clarify your ideal client, connect spiritually and strategically and attract dream clients without burning

CONCLUSION: THE REVOLUTION STARTS WITH YOU

out or selling out. Inside the community, you'll get lifetime access to:

- Weekly live calls
- Guest expert sessions
- A high-value training portal
- Aligned strategy support
- Spiritual integration tools
- An incredible community of proud entrepreneurs

You don't have to do this alone. Your people are waiting. Let's align, activate and attract – together. Go to https://helentudor.online/booklink1 or scan the QR code below for additional resources to support your Ideal Client Attraction journey and help you stay in alignment every step of the way:

Here you can take the free **Ideal Client Alignment Quiz** to find out whether your business is still a match for the you you've become or just a reflection of who you used to be. It's a fast, insightful diagnostic to help you reconnect with your strategy, soul and messaging.

You'll also find my gift to you – a free masterclass, **How To Attract Dream Clients Only.**

Acknowledgements

Thank you to everyone who helped me bring this book into the world: my husband and family for keeping me sane, my book guy, Joe Gregory, for getting me through it and my fantastic team, clients and audience for making it possible and cheering me on every step of the way. It takes a village; I just get to take the credit.

IDEAL CLIENT ATTRACTION

She's all about simple, actionable steps that move the needle. She wants you to win and she doesn't hold anything back.

Helen's superpower is co-creating Ideal Client Avatar maps so those she works with know exactly how to connect to their ideal client every day on a whole new level. This makes every tactic, strategy and funnel in the world work better. She shares all the secrets on how her clients are getting incredible results in their businesses – without working all the hours, burning out or dealing with difficult and demanding clients. Because business should feel *good*.

- https://helentudor.online
- https://facebook.com/helenctudor
- https://uk.linkedin.com/in/helentudor

The Author

Helen Tudor is a multi-award-winning entrepreneur who's built multiple six-figure businesses since starting online in 2016. She lives in Cheshire, UK, with her husband, their four teenage children, two slightly judgemental cats and a sausage dog called Dave.

Helen is an expert in helping incredible business owners align consistently with their most empowered selves, magnetise dream clients and create compelling offers that sell with ease. She's worked with tens of thousands of entrepreneurs through her coaching and programmes, and let's just say… she knows a thing or two about what works in the real world.